Contents

Let's Talk

Speaking and Listening Activities for Intermediate Students

Leo Jones

Robert Gallo
2342 - John Campbell
Lasalle, Qc. H8N 1C4
Tel:(514)367-3204 Fax:(514)367-3477
E-Mail: robertg@inforoute.net

CAMBRIDGE
UNIVERSITY PRESS

PUBLISHED BY THE PRESS SYNDICATE OF THE UNIVERSITY OF CAMBRIDGE
The Pitt Building, Trumpington Street, Cambridge CB2 1RP, United Kingdom

CAMBRIDGE UNIVERSITY PRESS
The Edinburgh Building, Cambridge CB2 2RU, United Kingdom
40 West 20th Street, New York, NY 10011-4211, USA
10 Stamford Road, Oakleigh, Melbourne 3166, Australia

© Cambridge University Press 1997

First published 1997

Printed in the United States of America

Typeset in Baskerville Book

ISBN 0 521 46753 5 Student's Book
ISBN 0 521 46752 7 Teacher's Manual
ISBN 0 521 46754 3 Cassettes

Book design; layout and design services: Don Williams

Students' introduction

Let's Talk is about communication. It is about listening to and understanding other people's ideas, and about sharing your ideas with your fellow students.

Be brave! Mistakes are an important part of the learning process, and by reaching for new language you will make progress, even if you sometimes make a mistake. Your partners and teacher will correct the mistakes that prevent you from communicating effectively.

There are 14 units in *Let's Talk*. Every unit includes these activities:

Pair work and Group work   These activities give you a chance to express your ideas and to hear the views of other students in the class. There are many pair and group work exercises in the book so that you can have plenty of speaking practice.

Listening exercises   In real life it is necessary to listen carefully in order to understand new information. The listening exercises in *Let's Talk* are based on authentic dialogues recorded on cassette, and each is accompanied by tasks for you to do as you listen. There are charts to fill in, notes to take, or "matching" exercises, where you decide on the right picture for each dialogue. You can discuss your reaction to the recorded dialogues in the pair or group work activities that follow most listenings.

Readings   Not every unit contains a reading selection, but where there *is* one, the reading will give you new information and ideas for discussion. Each reading is followed by discussion activities so that you can give your opinion about the information presented, or share information on a related topic.

Communication tasks   In each unit there is a communication task for you to do with a partner or group. These tasks give you a chance to practice your English in an informal setting. Sometimes you will be asked to look at photos and decide on a story for the photos. At other times you will be asked to exchange information with a partner or partners. Related communication tasks are on different pages so that you can't read each other's information. The instructions in each unit tell you which task to turn to at the back of the book.

Let's Talk will help you to enjoy using English while also widening your vocabulary and improving your grammatical accuracy. But you've read enough for the moment – now, let's talk!

Teacher's introduction

Let's Talk is a course in speaking and listening for intermediate students of American English. It can be used as the oral/aural component of any course that concentrates mainly on reading and writing skills. It can also be used as the basis for an intensive "refresher course" for learners who need to develop their fluency in English.

Each of the lessons focuses on a different topic, and the activities are designed to stimulate students to share their ideas, opinions, and experiences with each other. The topics are practical and interesting – the kinds of things that students want to talk about in any language – and the activities are realistic, motivating, and challenging.

The Cassettes that accompany the Student's Book feature interviews, conversations, news reports, and other interesting listening texts. Many of the recorded dialogues are unscripted to ensure that they reflect English as it is actually spoken in a variety of realistic situations. The speakers have a variety of authentic regional accents, and their speech contains the normal hesitations, pauses, and interruptions that naturally occur in spoken language.

Using *Let's Talk* in the classroom

Let's Talk consists of 14 units. Each unit contains 2–3 thematically related lessons. The lessons cover a wide range of topics, and it isn't necessary to do them in sequence. However, it is recommended that Lesson 1 be done first, because it helps students get to know each other, and serves as an introduction to the methods used throughout the book. Since the emphasis of the book is on generating discussion and promoting fluency, rather than on following an established syllabus, it is not absolutely necessary to complete every activity in the book. You may wish to select activities depending on the needs and interests of your students. For example, if your course has a strong emphasis on listening, you may wish to spend more time on the listening exercises and do fewer speaking activities.

One lesson will take about an hour to do, depending on
- how difficult a class finds the activities,
- how much interest is generated, and
- how many of the activities are selected.

Types of activities

Pair work and Group work

The activities in *Let's Talk* are most effective when learners work together in pairs or small groups of three to five students. The larger the class, the more these student-centered activities make sense because
- they give everyone a chance to speak,
- they allow meaningful conversations to develop, as opposed to isolated language practice, and
- they free learners from the fear of losing face in front of the whole class.

It's true that learners are more likely to make mistakes in less structured situations. However, it's much more productive for all class members to be participating in conversations, even if they are making mistakes, than for them to be listening to the teacher and answering questions one at a time in turn.

The teacher's role

While students are working in pairs or groups, move around the class and listen. If you think it would be helpful, join in occasionally and offer encouragement, advice, or suggestions. Make notes on any important mistakes you hear while you're walking around – but don't spend time actually correcting students' mistakes while they're trying to express themselves.

The teacher has three main responsibilities in involving students in pair or group work:
- getting things started (making sure everyone knows what to do and has the necessary vocabulary to do it);
- monitoring the groups at work and deciding when to stop the activity;
- leading a short follow-up discussion after each activity (answering questions, pointing out significant mistakes, and giving additional practice).

If your class does not have an even number of students, you may need to place some students in groups of three with two members of the group doing the same task. Rearrange groups and pairs frequently, so students are exposed to different speech styles and ideas. For some activities you may want to place outgoing learners together so they don't intimidate others. In other situations you may want the shy students paired with more outgoing partners so they can learn from them.

Don't worry if an activity fails to take off with a particular class. Open-ended exercises are inherently unpredictable. Bear in mind the attitudes and prejudices of your class when you are selecting activities, and be prepared to "sell" an activity to your students if you believe it to be a particularly worthwhile one. Some activities are easier than others. The ease in which students complete an activity may have more to do with the imaginations, opinions, experience, versatility, and knowledge they bring to class than the level of English required for the activity. Above all, though, the activities are designed to be enjoyable so students will be motivated to continue improving their English.

The use of native language

While using *Let's Talk*, students may lapse into their native language from time to time. When this happens, remind them that every member of the class has a common aim: to improve his or her English. One of the guiding principles of this course is to foster a spirit of cooperation and friendship in the class. Students should think of themselves as a team, with each member of the team having a part to play in the success of the course.

Grammar and mistakes

Although learners using *Let's Talk* should already have a basic knowledge of English grammar, they will still make mistakes. Accuracy is an important aspect of language learning and should never be ignored, but it is more important for students to be able to communicate effectively. Many grammatical mistakes don't seriously affect communication. No student should be corrected every time he or she makes a mistake. If that happened, many students would become inhibited and afraid to speak at all! Actually, mistakes are an essential indicator of what still needs to be learned. On the basis of the mistakes you overhear, together with the types of questions students ask you, you can plan any additional practice your class may require.

If you would like to supplement the fluency exercises in *Let's Talk* with grammar practice, I recommend using *Communicative Grammar Practice*, published by Cambridge University Press. This text covers the main problem areas in grammar that intermediate-level students encounter.

Communication tasks

Every unit of *Let's Talk* contains at least one communication task. The purpose of the communication tasks is to simulate real-life conversations. One characteristic of everyday conversation is that when we talk to another person, we don't usually know exactly what information the other person has or what the other person is going to say. This gap in knowledge is called an "information gap." The communication tasks in *Let's Talk* create information gaps that exist in typical conversations.

In the communication tasks, students are directed to separate sections at the back of the book. Each person is given a different set of information and can't see his or her partner's information. Students need to find out what their partners know and tell their partners what they know. You will find that students will be motivated by the desire to exchange information in the realistic situations presented. In this way, information gaps will be created and bridged – and meaningful communication will take place.

As students perform the communication tasks, you can go around the room and assist them with vocabulary and instructions.

There is a brief description of each communication task in its related Procedure section in the Teacher's Manual. For quick reference, a complete index of the communication tasks can be found on page 113 of this Teacher's Manual.

Listening activities

The listening activities give students practice listening to authentic English conversations and develop skills that make them better listeners. Tasks are designed to help students understand the main points of the conversation. Students are discouraged from listening to every single word and worrying about what they don't understand.

Listening is a skill that requires students to concentrate on what they *do* understand. For example, if a speaker does not pronounce a word clearly, there's no point in having the students worry about what the word is if it means that he or she stops listening to what the speaker says next – just as in real life you have to ignore the words you don't understand and concentrate on the main points that are being made. It would be impossible for students to acquire this skill if the only English they were exposed to was slow and simple. Using the *Let's Talk* recordings and accompanying listening activities will help the students acquire this essential listening skill.

Note that the transcripts of the recorded material are printed in the Teacher's Manual but not printed in the Student's Book. If the students had transcripts to refer to, they might use them as a "crutch" while listening to the recordings, and this wouldn't help them to acquire the skill of understanding real-life conversations. From time to time, however, you may decide to photocopy a transcript from the Teacher's Manual, but you shouldn't do this too often.

Read/listen activities

The Student's Book contains authentic newspaper and magazine articles presented as "read/listen" activities. Students read a short text that has a number of words missing from it. Their task is to guess the missing words, and then listen to confirm their guesses. This kind of exercise forces students to read the text very carefully and think about the ideas it contains. The recorded reading also demonstrates how the words are pronounced and helps students to make more sense of the text. Most of the read/listen activities are followed by comprehension exercises and discussion questions that give students a chance to react to the reading.

Vocabulary

As they work through *Let's Talk*, students will be learning more and more vocabulary. Some vocabulary items are presented in special vocabulary exercises, while others occur in context in the recordings and the reading texts.

In this Teacher's Manual, the teaching notes for each activity include a glossary that defines the important new vocabulary students will come across in that activity. In general, difficult vocabulary items are listed; however, for the recordings, only the words that are key to understanding the main ideas are defined. The definitions reflect the meanings of the words in the contexts in which they're used in *Let's Talk*, rather than their meanings in universal contexts. You may need to consult a dictionary for complete definitions and further examples of the words used in different contexts.

Presenting vocabulary

It is important to limit definition of vocabulary to those words that are essential to the task. Students can often complete an activity successfully without understanding every word. In fact, learners should be encouraged to develop a tolerance for ambiguity so they don't panic when they see an unfamiliar word. By focusing on essential vocabulary only, you can use your in-class time more efficiently.

Before presenting the definition of a word, ask students if they can explain the word. If no one can, give the meaning provided in the Teacher's Manual or ask students to look up the word in a good learner's dictionary. Whenever possible, encourage students to guess the meaning of a word from its context, an important reading and listening skill. At first, students may need your guidance, but as their skill develops, they will be able to do this on their own. Explain that guessing the meaning of a word from its context involves

- looking in the text or at the other words in the vocabulary box for clues about the word,
- thinking about what they know about similar words, and
- using their knowledge of the world.

For an example of how you can provide guidance, look at page 8 in the Student's Book. Students may not know the meaning of the word *appetizer* in Activity A. You can lead them to guess the definition by naming some common appetizers that they might be familiar with (for example, shrimp cocktail, a small salad) and asking them when they'd eat those dishes. If someone answers, "at the beginning of a meal," you can say, "That's right, appetizers are eaten before a meal." If students work out the meaning for themselves, they're more likely to remember the new word.

Students may ask about other words in each lesson that are not listed in the glossary for a particular activity. You should preview the activities and the transcripts of the recorded material and be prepared to answer questions about any potentially difficult words. Alternatively, you can have students look the words up in their dictionaries.

You may discover that some of the vocabulary introduced in the *Let's Talk* Student's Book are low-frequency words. For example, in Communication Task 3 on page C-3, *bungee jumping* and *hang gliding* are given as examples of a person's hobbies. These expressions are not often used in everyday conversation, but students must get used to encountering and coping with such low-frequency words. They should try to understand them, and in many cases they will be able to guess their meanings from the context. Conversely, you may want to point out commonly used words for students feeling overwhelmed by the vocabulary or with limited time to study.

In some exercises (for example, at the bottom of page 8 of the Student's Book), students are expected to use dictionaries to look up the meanings of unfamiliar words. Any kind of dictionary is suitable for these exercises, even a small bilingual dictionary, but you may want to recommend that your students use an English-to-English dictionary.

Review puzzles

There are five puzzle pages in the Student's Book. Each one reviews vocabulary introduced in the preceding lessons. Some of the crossword puzzle-type clues are more difficult than others, and students should realize that it's sometimes best to skip a difficult clue and come back to it later. The puzzle pages shouldn't present any serious problems since many students will have had experience with this kind of puzzle in their own language.

Most students will prefer to do the puzzle on their own at their own speed. Allow time for students to check their answers in the next classroom session. However, if you have some spare time in class, students will enjoy working on the puzzles together in pairs.

Follow-up activities

In some lessons, extra activities are suggested in the Teacher's Manual for use at your discretion. The follow-up activities are discussion tasks that are most appropriate if your students have become very interested in one of the topics, and you think it's worth spending more time on that particular lesson.

Writing activities

Although *Let's Talk* is predominantly a course in speaking and listening skills, you may want your students to do some writing exercises as part of the course. To facilitate this, there is a suggested writing activity at the end of many of the lessons in the Teacher's Manual. To do the activity, the students will need to spend some time preparing in class. The written work should be assigned as homework. Here is a suggested procedure:

1. Begin by brainstorming ideas with the class, making notes of the best ideas on the board.
2. Put the students into pairs and have them make notes on what they're going to write. (Students make their own notes, but offer their partners support and encouragement.)
3. Have students do the written assignment at their own speed outside of class.
4. Have students show their completed work to the same student they made notes with in step 2. The students suggest minor improvements and react to what they read.
5. Ask students to hand the improved work to you for comments.
6. Comment on the written work. When commenting, try to maintain a balance between accuracy and expression. In other words, too many corrections may dampen a student's desire to communicate.
7. Hand back the work and go around the class making sure everyone reads their corrections and has a chance to respond to the corrections.

The "To the student" page

Before you begin Lesson 1, make sure the students understand the contents of the "To the student" page in the Student's Book. It's important that the ideas expressed on this page don't come as too much of a surprise to the students when they begin work on Lesson 1.

About this Teacher's Manual

For each lesson in the Student's Book, the Teacher's Manual contains
- vocabulary glossaries listing important words that the students will encounter in the activities,
- procedures suggesting how to use the material,
- answers or sample answers,
- transcripts of any recorded material,
- a follow-up activity (in some lessons), and
- a writing activity (in some lessons).

Please don't feel constrained by the suggested teaching procedures for each activity. You may be able to think of better ways of doing some activities with your class, according to their needs and interests.

I do hope you enjoy using *Let's Talk*!

Leo Jones

1 What kind of person are you?

Unit 1, *Getting to know you*, consists of Lessons 1–3. It focuses on introducing oneself, talking about personalities, and getting to know someone better.

This lesson introduces some of the words and phrases that are used to talk about characters and personalities. Students should be encouraged to share their views on this subject – though some students may be justifiably skeptical about some of the ideas presented here (for example, the idea of judging someone's personality based on his or her favorite color). Encourage your students to discuss the ideas and explain why they agree or disagree with them.

The activities in this lesson will work both with students who already know one another and students who are together for the first time.

Since some of your students may not have worked in pairs or in groups before, it may be necessary to demonstrate how these discussion activities might proceed. You can do this by acting out various conversations with your more confident students. Make it clear that the activities in this book are "fluency activities," in which the emphasis is on communicating ideas rather than avoiding mistakes. They should try to keep talking, asking for help with vocabulary only when absolutely necessary.

If some of your students are speaking extensively in their native language, stop the activity and tell them that they *can* manage the discussion in English. Students need to remember that the primary goal of the activity is to improve their English-speaking skills.

Activity A

page 2

Vocabulary

The words a particular student needs to express his or her opinions and ideas may not be in the Student's Book, so the questions the student asks about words are an important factor in developing his or her vocabulary.

stressful   worrying
casual clothes   clothes worn at home or for leisure activities
formal clothes   clothes worn for a special occasion
deserted   empty (of people)
in order of preference   starting with your favorite and ending with the one you like least

1 Pair work

1. Begin by looking at the pictures with the whole class. Ask students to suggest sentences that describe what's happening in each photo. Encourage everyone to make suggestions, and offer them advice on vocabulary and ways of rephrasing what they've said. Encourage students to express their ideas without worrying about making mistakes.

2. Brainstorm vocabulary that might be used to describe what the various people are doing.

procedure continues on next page

3. Have students look at the words in the box to the left of the photos. The pairs of words are opposites. Ask students if they understand all the words. Encourage students to say which words can be used to describe each picture.

4. Divide the class into pairs. If you have an odd number of students, one "pair" should consist of three students. Ask students to talk about the photos, following the instructions in the Student's Book. Give them two or three minutes to do this.

2 Pair work

1. Have students remain in the same pairs for this activity.

2. The speech balloon suggests some useful phrases that can be used when talking about the photos. Demonstrate how to use the phrases by talking about your own preferences, but be careful not to give the idea that your preferences are the "right answers."

3. Make sure students understand that they are to indicate their preferences by numbering the photos. Have each student do this individually before talking with his or her partner.

4. While they're discussing their preferences, go around the class listening to each pair. Be ready to help with vocabulary but don't interrupt the conversations to correct mistakes, as this might discourage students.

5. Tell students that any pair that finishes early should try to talk more about the photos. Point out that asking "Why?" would be a good way of encouraging their partners to say more.

6. Reassemble the class and ask two or three students to explain which photos they liked the best and the least.

Activity B

pages 2–3

Vocabulary

personality   character; the type of person you are, shown by the way you behave, feel, and think
outdoors   outside, not in a building
the environment   the air, water, and land around us
to do your own thing   to be independent
to have a quick temper   to become angry easily
to plan ahead   to decide in advance what you are going to do

1 Pair work

1. Arrange students with a different partner than they were with for Activity A. This is intended to be a lighthearted activity. Students should be encouraged to be skeptical about the judgments suggested in the chart.

2. Ask students to follow the instructions in the Student's Book. You might also want to suggest that they put the colors in order of personal preference from 1 (favorite) to 9 (least favorite).

2 Pair work

1. Have students remain in the same pairs.
2. Explain that the chart comes from a magazine. Point out that the speech balloon below the chart suggests some ways of reacting to the ideas in the chart.
3. Have students read the chart and discuss their reactions to it. Many of them will disagree with the judgments, and that should generate some discussion.
4. Conclude the activity with a short class discussion about the students' reactions.

Activity C

page 3

1 Pair work

1. Arrange the class into groups of four or five. Then subdivide each group into two pairs (or a pair and a group of three).
2. Have the pairs follow the instructions in the Student's Book. They should try to guess the preferences of each student in the other pair, either based on what they discovered about them earlier in the lesson or by looking at them (for example, one student may be dressed entirely in black or have a bright pink backpack).

2 Join another pair

1. Have the pairs recombine into their original groups of four (or five).
2. Draw your students' attention to the speech balloon, which shows a possible way of starting a conversation about favorite places and colors. You may also want to demonstrate how the conversation might continue.
3. Have the groups review what they discussed in Activities A and B. This step recycles some of the vocabulary they used before and helps them develop confidence. Go around the class listening to as many groups as you can. Don't interrupt or make corrections, but do answer any questions students may have.
4. Ask the class if they have any questions, particularly concerning vocabulary.

Activity D

page 3

Communication task 👥

Vocabulary

adjective   a word that describes somebody or something
shy   nervous and uncomfortable with other people
outgoing   friendly and finding it easy and enjoyable to be with other people
messy   untidy and rather dirty
scribble   write something quickly or carelessly

Procedure

You will need to explain the purpose of this activity since this is the students' first communication task. Be sure to look at the two tasks (Task 1 on page C-2 and Task 12 on page C-8) before the lesson so that you can answer any questions that may arise.

procedure continues on next page

1. Explain that there is going to be an "information gap" (see Introduction, p. ix). Explain to students that since the goal of this kind of activity is to simulate a real-life conversation (where unexpected things happen), they should not look at their partner's page.

2. Demonstrate how the task works by asking three or four students one of the questions in Task 12 (for example, "When you shop, do you usually make a list of what you need before you go out, or do you buy whatever looks good?"). Ask the other students to suggest what a student's answer tells them about his or her personality.

3. Arrange the class into pairs. One student in each pair follows the instructions given in Task 1 on page C-2 and the other follows the instructions given in Task 12 on page C-8. Each member of the pair has a different questionnaire, which he or she uses to learn more about the other person's personality.

4. The first student asks his or her partner all the questions in Task 1. Then he or she uses adjectives from the box to evaluate the partner's personality. The speech balloon suggests some useful patterns. Go around the class listening to as many pairs as you can. Don't interrupt or make corrections, but do answer any questions they may have.

5. The second student should follow the same procedure, using the questions in Task 12. The speech balloon suggests how to begin the evaluation.

6. Ask two or three pairs of students to tell the rest of the class what they discovered about their partners.

7. Ask the class if they have any questions, particularly about vocabulary. Inquire if they were able to keep the conversations going in English without resorting to their native language. If they were, congratulate them and ask them how they accomplished it. If they were not, tell them that with more practice they will soon be able to carry on conversations entirely in English.

8. Before the next class, ask students to look at Lesson 2 in their books.

2 Breaking the ice

The expressions presented in this lesson are useful "icebreakers." Initiating a conversation with a stranger is often the hardest part of having a conversation. In fact, students may assume that they are the only ones who don't know what to say when in reality the stranger may be even shyer than they are! It's a shame if an opportunity for learners to communicate in English is missed because they don't know how to start a conversation.

This lesson practices starting a conversation with a stranger. Rather than presenting ready-made conversational gambits, encourage students to develop and share their own ideas. Original ideas promote class discussion that is valuable even if the prospects of meeting English-speaking people may seem to be a remote possibility to your students.

Activity A
page 4

Vocabulary

icebreaker   a remark used to start a conversation with someone you do not know
expression   words used in a particular situation
elevator   a small room that moves people up or down in tall buildings
coworker   a person who works with you
a tough teacher   a demanding or strict teacher
out of service   not working
emergency button   the button you press for help in a dangerous situation
to walk around in circles   to be lost; not to know where you are going
a (city) block   an area of land with buildings on it and streets on all sides
document   a piece of paper with printed information on it

1 Pair work

1. Draw students' attention to the explanation of the lesson title at the top of the page. Ask students if they have a similar expression in their own language.
2. You may want students to brainstorm ideas for the first picture.
3. While students are suggesting ideas, go around the room offering advice and answering questions.

Sample answers

Students will hear different icebreakers in the recording.
   1. Hello. Are you enjoying this class?
   2. Oh, no! The elevator seems to have stopped.
   3. Excuse me, are you lost?
   4. Can I help you?

2 Listen

1. Some students may not be accustomed to hearing unsimplified English conversations like the ones in this course. Reassure students that it isn't necessary to understand every word that is spoken. Tell them that they should concentrate on identifying the icebreakers and trying to get the main idea of each conversation. (Note that the recorded conversations also act as models for the kind of conversations students will be acting out in Activity B2 on the next page.)

2. Play the tape, pausing it between each conversation. Give everyone time to compare the conversation with their own ideas, and answer any questions that arise. Make it clear that the conversations are examples of what could be said in each situation rather than fixed dialogues that have to be memorized.

Transcript   2 minutes 30 seconds

One. It's the first week of class.
WOMAN 1: Hi.
WOMAN 2: Hi.
WOMAN 1: How do you like this class?
WOMAN 2: Oh, I really like it.
WOMAN 1: Yeah, me too, so far.
WOMAN 2: It's a little bit hard.
WOMAN 1: Yeah, I had the same teacher last year. She is a little tough.
WOMAN 2: Oh, you did? (Yeah.) Um . . . Are her tests hard?
WOMAN 1: Her tests aren't that bad if you keep up with the reading . . .

Two. You're stuck in an elevator.
MAN 1: Uh-oh. . . . Looks like there's a problem.
MAN 2: Yeah. . . . Does this happen all the time?
MAN 1: Yeah, I'm afraid so. Last Friday this elevator was out of service all day long.
MAN 2: Do you think I should press the emergency button?
MAN 1: No, let's just wait a minute or two first. It may start by itself again.
MAN 2: OK. . . . Do you work here?

Three. You see a tourist who needs help.
WOMAN 1: Hi. Excuse me, . . . um . . . do you need any help?
WOMAN 2: Oh, yes, I do. I've been walking around in circles. I . . . I can't seem to find the train station.
WOMAN 1: Oh, well, I'm going in that direction. You can walk with me. I'll show you where it is.
WOMAN 2: Oh, are you sure it's no trouble? (Oh, yeah.) I can't read this map.
WOMAN 1: Really, it's no trouble at all. I mean, it's only a couple of blocks from here . . .

Four. A coworker needs help sending a fax.
WOMAN: Excuse me, do you need a hand?
MAN: Oh, yes, please. I haven't used one like this before.
WOMAN: Oh, it's . . . it's really quite easy. All you have to do is place the document here.
MAN: Here? OK.
WOMAN: Yeah. And then you dial the number.
MAN: Right. That's it? That's . . .
WOMAN: And . . . no . . . then you press the green button.
MAN: This one? OK. Great, thanks a lot.
WOMAN: You're welcome. I don't think I've seen you around here before.
MAN: No, you haven't. I'm new. I just started to work here last week.
WOMAN: Oh, really? Welcome . . .

3 Listen again 📼

1. Play the conversations again (the four conversations are repeated on the tape) and have students complete the chart. They will understand more of each conversation as they hear it for the second time.

2. Ask students to compare their answers in pairs. If there is a lot of disagreement about which answers are right, play the conversations again before you reveal the correct answers to the class.

3. If there is time, play each conversation again and ask students to comment on how the people in the conversations reacted to the icebreakers. The advantage of a third listening is that this time students will understand even more of the conversations, though probably still not everything.

Answers

See the previous page for a transcript of this activity.

	Yes	No	Conversation #
1. Do you need a hand?	✔		4
2. Is this seat taken?		✔	
3. How do you like this class?	✔		1
4. Does this happen all the time?	✔		2
5. Do you need any help?	✔		3
6. Where do you live?		✔	

Activity B

page 5

1 Pair work

1. Actively encourage pairs of students to share their ideas. Even if the activity isn't proceeding very smoothly at first, don't stop it. If some pairs really seem "stuck," allow them to work with others in groups of three or four. The open-ended nature of this activity may be challenging for some students.

2. Reassemble the class and ask some (or all) of the pairs to report back their best ideas to the class. Make it clear that there are no correct answers. The following sample answers are given as suggestions only, and your students may have much better ideas.

Sample answers

For the photo on the top left

May I borrow your newspaper? (asked of unused portion of paper)
Is today's weather forecast in the paper?
Are you going to . . . on vacation or on business?
Do you travel a lot?

answers continue on next page

Activity B

*page 5
continued*

For the photo on the right

Would you like some coffee?
Are you new here?
What did you think of the meeting?
Where do they keep the cream and sugar?

For the photo on the bottom left

Would you like more coffee?
It's a great party, isn't it?
How do you know (host of the party)?
Are you enjoying the party?

For the chart

Situation	Icebreaker
at a sports event	Do you come to these games often? How long have you been a . . . fan?
waiting for a bus	I wonder how long we'll have to wait. Have you been waiting long?
on a bus or train	Do you know when we'll get to . . . ? Does this bus/train stop at . . . ?

2 Pair work

1. Arrange students into new pairs for this activity so they can more easily pretend to be strangers. Make sure to allow enough time for students to converse, as the goal of this activity is for each pair's conversation to move past the icebreaking stage and find topics in common to talk about.

2. Encourage students to be polite and friendly. As an example, demonstrate how asking someone "Are you new here?" too abruptly may sound overly aggressive. Demonstrate this same question again, but in a much more welcoming tone. Emphasize to students that they should avoid one-word answers: Being responsive encourages the other person to be equally responsive and friendly.

3. Point out the expressions in the speech balloon. Tell students that they can use these icebreakers as they act out the situation(s).

4. If there's time, students should act out *several* situations, with each taking a turn at being the person who begins the conversation. Perhaps rearrange the pairs again so that they can have a third attempt with a different "stranger."

5. Ask students to think of a situation in which they had the chance to make contact with a stranger but didn't. Ask students what they could have said to make contact and if they regret not doing so.

6. Before the next class, ask students to read the article on page 6 of the Student's Book and guess the missing words.

3 Getting to know more about you . . .

Vocabulary

impression   the way you look or seem to other people
psychologist   a person who studies the human mind, emotions, and behavior
facial expressions   movements of your face that show how you feel
body language   gestures and movements of your body that show how you feel
eye contact   the moment when two people look at each other at the same time
tone of voice   the loudness, intonation, and speed of your voice (that shows how you feel)
message   a piece of information that is communicated
aggressive   threatening; ready to attack
supportive   helpful; understanding

1 Read/listen

1. Ask your students to read the article and guess the missing words before coming to class. If it is not possible to assign the reading for homework, allow plenty of class time for students to complete the task.

2. Make it clear to students if they guess wrong they haven't necessarily made a mistake. (Guessing the missing words in the article encourages students to read it carefully and focus on meaning.) In most cases, there is more than one possible answer for each missing word.

3. Ask everyone to read the article and guess the missing words. (Students can work together or alone to complete this task.)

4. Play the tape while the students listen and check their answers. The missing words are printed in bold type in the transcript that follows.

5. Ask students if they have any questions about "wrong guesses" they may have made, and help them decide which of their words, while not on the tape, are plausible answers.

6. Have the students highlight any vocabulary in the passage they would like to remember.

Transcript and answers   2 minutes

Missing words are in bold type.

First Impressions

According to psychologists, people form first impressions based first on how you look, then on how you **sound**, and finally on what you say.

Your physical appearance – how you **look** – makes up fifty-five percent of a first impression. This includes facial expressions, body language, and eye contact, as well as **clothing** and general appearance.

The way you sound makes up **thirty-eight** percent of the first impression. This includes how fast or slowly, loudly or softly you **speak**, and your tone of voice. People listen

transcript continues on next page

to your tone of voice and decide whether you sound **friendly** or unfriendly, interested or bored, and happy or sad. What you say – the actual words you use – counts for only seven percent of the message.

People form their first impressions within **ten** seconds of meeting you. And first impressions don't change easily. If someone gets the wrong impression of you, it can take a long time to change his or her mind.

Sometimes it is hard to make sure that you always give a **good** first impression. One problem is that in different parts of the world, the same behavior may give people a different **impression**. In some countries,

looking directly at someone is polite. It shows you are alert and confident. In other countries, looking directly at someone is considered aggressive. It is more polite to look **away**. Standing close to someone is considered friendly and supportive in some countries. In others, you are expected to keep your **distance**.

Giving a good first impression depends on many things. Everyone **behaves** in different ways, but when you're not sure you're giving a good impression, the best thing to do is ask yourself, "What would *I* think of someone who acted this way?"

2 Pair work

1. Arrange the class into an even number of pairs so they can easily combine into small groups in the next activity.

2. As they do the activity, students will discover that their responses will vary. However, some things on the list do seem rather unlikely in any situation, unless a person is meeting a relative or someone he or she already knows.

3. After the pairs have discussed the list, ask them to report to the whole class to see if there are any disagreements. Ask students if they think they've found any universal conclusions that constitute "safe behavior" (behavior that will give a good impression in any situation).

3 Join another pair

1. Combine the pairs into groups of four (or five). Students may find that they are repeating some of the same ideas, but this is intentional: The activity will develop confidence and fluency.

2. You might want to ask the class to suggest some other things they *would* do during the beginning (and at the end) of a first-time conversation.

Follow-up activity

Ask the class to suggest other examples of behavior and personal characteristics that may influence the impression a person makes. Here are some examples that may come up (be prepared to discuss and/or explain any new vocabulary items):

facial expressions	smiling, blinking, frowning, looking someone straight in the eye, looking down
noises	sighing, yawning, clicking a pen, tapping fingers, giggling, sniffing, humming, whistling
body language	crossing legs, folding arms, standing up, putting hands in pockets

clothes and accessories	uniforms, casual clothes, formal clothes, ties, open-necked shirts, shorts, short skirts, jewelry
appearance	well-groomed hands, long hair, very short hair, beards, mustaches, tattoos, pierced ears (noses, etc.)

Vocabulary

assignment   homework
political science   the study of politics
Danish   the language of Denmark
confused   mixed up in your mind
disaster   a very bad situation
money management   ways of organizing and investing money
overseas   across the ocean in another country
adoringly   in a loving way

1 Listen

The purpose of this activity is to focus students' attention on the main points that are made, not to quiz them on what they understood.

1. Before playing the tape, ask students to read the questions. Tell students that although they may hear more than one answer for some of the questions, they only need to write one answer for each question.

2. Play the tape, stopping between the two interviews so students have time to discuss their answers.

3. Replay the tape if necessary. At the same time, reassure your students that being able to answer the questions proves that they've understood all the main points that the speakers made.

4. Ask students to compare their answers with a partner before you review them as a class.

Answers

1. English, science, history
2. he likes the teacher; the teacher makes it exciting; the teacher makes it fun
3. go to college; study political science
4. become a lawyer; do something he could make some money at

5. her language classes (French, Spanish, and Danish)
6. Spanish
7. with a bank (maybe abroad) or at the UN (United Nations)
8. France (because the food is great) or Denmark (because she met someone who told her how nice it was)

see next page for transcript

Transcript and answers   3 minutes 30 seconds

Possible answers for Activity B2 are in bold type. The two interviews are recorded twice on the tape.

First, Michael.

INTERVIEWER: So, Michael, **what's your favorite class?**

MICHAEL: In school?

INTERVIEWER: Yeah.

MICHAEL: Uh . . . I really . . . I really like English, you know, and . . . um . . . science. Science is good, . . . um . . . history. Hmm. I like most of the classes I'm taking this year.

INTERVIEWER: Mm-hmm. **Why do you really like English?**

MICHAEL: Um . . . Well, I li- I like literature. (Uh-huh.) I like . . . I like to read, and . . . um . . .

INTERVIEWER: Well, that's good.

MICHAEL: Yeah. And we've had a lot of good assignments this year. We read some Dickens and . . . um . . . some good stuff.

INTERVIEWER: **What about in history? What do you like about history?**

MICHAEL: Um . . . My teacher's really – uh . . . he's an excellent teacher in history class. And . . . uh . . . you know, he makes it exciting, he makes it fun for us.

INTERVIEWER: Yeah, that really helps, doesn't it?

MICHAEL: Yeah, because I've had some teachers – they've just, you know, they've been pretty bad.

INTERVIEWER: **Do you have trouble remembering dates or anything?**

MICHAEL: Yeah, yeah, the dates are probably the hardest part, but (Yeah, me too.) if you study you get them, though.

INTERVIEWER: Good!

MICHAEL: You know, if you study. Yeah. It helps.

INTERVIEWER: **What do you want to do when you finish school?**

MICHAEL: Well, . . . hmm . . . hopefully, I'll go to college, you know. I'm applying now, so, you know, we'll find out this summer, you know, what I get into.

INTERVIEWER: **Do you have a specific . . . um . . . course that you want to take?**

MICHAEL: Uh . . . I'd like to study . . . uh . . . politics, (Uh-huh.) political science, you know, possibly law at some point.

INTERVIEWER: **So what do you want to be?**

MICHAEL: Uh . . . I'm not sure, I'm not sure. I'd like to be a lawyer, (Uh-huh.) but . . . uh . . . I know how hard that is, so . . . I don't know. Just something I could make some money at, hopefully.

Now, Amy.

INTERVIEWER: So, Amy, which classes do you enjoy the most in college?

AMY: Well, I think . . . um . . . my language classes are probably my favorites right now.

INTERVIEWER: Mm-hmm. Which ones are you taking?

AMY: I'm taking three. I'm studying French, Spanish, and Danish right now.

INTERVIEWER: Uh-huh. Why? What made you pick those three?

AMY: Well, . . . um . . . I've always loved languages – I thought (**Uh-huh.**) Spanish would be the most useful.

INTERVIEWER: **Uh-huh.**

AMY: Uh . . . French is the most beautiful, I think.

INTERVIEWER: **Mm-hmm.**

AMY: And . . . uh . . . I met . . . uh . . . someone from Denmark a couple of years ago and loved the language, and I decided to study that, too.

INTERVIEWER: That's terrific. (Yeah.) Do you ever get them confused in your mind while you're studying?

AMY: Sometimes. (**Yeah?**) Yeah, sometimes I mix them up, and it's a disaster!

INTERVIEWER: Ha-ha-ha. What other classes are you taking in school?

AMY: Um . . . I'm taking a money management class right **(Oh.)** now. That's . . . uh . . . that's not bad. I thought it would be just awful, but it's . . . it's really kind of interesting.

INTERVIEWER: How did you land in money management?

AMY: Well, my parents thought it would be **(Ah.)** a good idea.

INTERVIEWER: Aha. (Yeah.) So are you hoping to work out some way to combine the two disciplines?

AMY: Yeah, I'm hoping that I'll be able to get a good position . . . um . . . with a business, maybe with a bank . . . uh . . . abroad or . . . **(Mm-hmm.)** or here.

INTERVIEWER: **Mm-hmm.**

AMY: Um . . . There's also the possibility of working at the UN, which **(Sure.)** would be great.

INTERVIEWER: Sure. Uh . . . If . . . if your work takes you overseas, where would you like to live?

AMY: I think France.

INTERVIEWER: **Yeah? Why?**

AMY: Yeah. The food! **(Ha-ha-ha.)** The food is great!

INTERVIEWER: OK. Um . . . Uh . . . Any other country that you'd like to live in other than France?

AMY: Um . . . I think Denmark, too.

INTERVIEWER: **Mm-hmm. How come?**

AMY: Uh . . . This . . . this . . . uh . . . this fellow that I met . . . um . . . uh . . . spoke so . . . so adoringly of his **(Mm-hmm.)** country. Um . . . I- I'd like to . . . uh . . . I'd like to see what it's like there.

INTERVIEWER: Mm-hmm. Well, I wish you luck.

AMY: Thanks very much.

INTERVIEWER: Sounds very exciting.

AMY: Thank you.

2 Listen again 🔲

1. Tell students the purpose of this activity is to make them aware of some of the techniques they can use to encourage another person to say more.

2. As you play the tape, pause it occasionally to allow the students time to write their answers. (The transcript and answers to this activity begin on the previous page.)

3 Join a partner

1. Have students compare the notes they've made.

2. There may be some dispute over the spelling of noises like *Mm* and *Uh-huh*. Tell everyone that, as these are not words, the spelling is not important.

Activity C

page 7

1 Pair work

1. Ask students to follow the directions and discuss the questions in the speech balloon.

2. Bring the class back together and discuss the nature of these questions. After looking at the questions in the speech balloon, the students should be able to work out for themselves that a *yes/no* question is less likely to encourage someone to answer at length than a *Wh*-question. You might want to point out that if someone is *really* determined not to say much, the first two questions on the right could be answered with short responses such as "Tokyo" or "It's OK."

procedure continues on next page

3. At the conclusion of the class discussion, make sure everyone understands the distinction between open questions and closed questions (left-hand column). (Open questions often ask for a person's opinions, feelings, or thoughts about something, whereas closed questions generally ask for a specific piece of information.)

2 Work alone

Some students may need a little help, so go around the class offering advice and suggestions.

Sample answers

What do you do in your free time?
What sports do you enjoy?
What are/were your favorite classes in college/school?
Where do/did you go to school?
What do you think about . . . (something that's in the news now) ?

3 Join a partner

1. Try to match students who don't normally sit together so they can find out more about each other.

2. If there's time, rearrange students again so they can talk with a different partner. For students at this level "getting it right and doing it better" can be very reassuring. Presenting familiar information more than once allows students to work on fluency.

3. Ask students to report to the class about one interesting thing they found out about their partner (for example, "I found out that Maria has six brothers," or "I found out that Yoshi plays the guitar.")

Follow-up activity

Discuss the use of personal questions. Write the following questions on the board or simply read them aloud, and ask students to identify those questions that they would *not* ask someone they just met.

How old are you?
Do you have a girlfriend/boyfriend?
What do you like to do in your
  free time?
Where do/did you go to school?
What is your greatest ambition?
How much do you earn?
What's your favorite color?

What are you going to do when you
  finish your education?
Are you married?
What kind of car do you drive?
Do you live with your family?
Are you happy?
What's your job?
Do you enjoy your work?

Writing activity

Give students the following directions for a writing task:

Think about the person you talked to in Activity C3. Write a short paragraph (about 50 words) that tells what you found out about him or her.

4 How do you cook that?

Unit 2, *Food and cooking*, consists of Lessons 4–5. It focuses on favorite foods, recipes, menus, and restaurants.

page 8

Vocabulary

appetizer   a dish that is eaten before the main course
dessert   a sweet food, such as cake or ice cream, that is eaten after the main course
category   a group of things that share a common feature

Other important vocabulary includes the words in the box at the bottom of page 8 of the Student's Book.

1 Pair work

1. Arrange the class into an even number of pairs so students can easily combine into small groups in the next activity.

2. Be prepared to offer students help with vocabulary as they fill in the chart. Encourage them to explain *why* they like the foods they like.

Sample answers

What's your favorite . . . ?
   hot drink: espresso or coffee
   cold drink: orange juice
   main course: grilled steak
   appetizer: avocado with shrimp
   vegetable: spinach
   dessert: chocolate mousse
   foreign food: sushi
   snack: peanut butter and jelly sandwich
What do you like to cook? pasta
What's your "specialty"? spaghetti with meatballs
What's your favorite restaurant? Planet Hollywood

2 Join another pair

1. Combine the pairs into groups of four (or five).

2. Have students continue discussing favorite foods and foods they don't like. The questions are very open-ended and may lead to all sorts of interesting revelations.

3. Allow students plenty of time for this discussion. Circulate around the class, eavesdropping and encouraging your students.

3 Group work

1. Have students remain in the same groups. This activity encourages students to share their knowledge of English vocabulary. If your students have fluorescent highlighters available, they can use them to mark any new expressions. Doing so will make it easier for students to notice them when they review the lesson.

procedure continues on next page

Activity A

*page 8
continued*

2. If necessary, go through the words in the list, saying them out loud so that your students can hear them pronounced correctly. Ask students to repeat any of the words that they're likely to find particularly difficult.

3. You can expect many of these vocabulary items to be new words for your students. Individual students will circle (or mark) different words, so it's important that members in each group pool their knowledge.

4. Have students use their dictionaries to look up any words that they don't know, or, if you prefer, they could ask you to explain them.

5. Finally, make sure that students add two more words to each list.

Sample answers

ways of preparing food: chop, mix, spread
ways of cooking: boil, barbecue, panfry
equipment: wok, food processor, rice cooker, toaster, cutting board, knife, spoon

Activity B

page 9

Vocabulary

flounder   a small, flat fish
to marinate   to leave food in a liquid so that the food absorbs the flavors of the liquid before cooking
julienned   cut into very thin strips
to garnish   to place something on top of food to decorate it
seasoned   flavored with salt and pepper and perhaps herbs and spices
aside   to one side
to drain   to allow the liquid to flow away
smooth   creamy and without lumps
bubble   small balls of air in a liquid
crispy food   food that has been fried or toasted so it is hard or crunchy
gravy   a sauce made from the juices of cooked meat

1 Listen

1. Begin by asking students to read through the list of ingredients. They will hear many of these words on the tape. A lot of vocabulary in this activity may be new to students. If you attempt to explain all the vocabulary before students listen to the tape, you'll use up a lot of valuable class time. As students complete the activity, they should be able to guess the meaning of most unfamiliar words from context. Be prepared, however, to answer questions about vocabulary at any time during this activity.

2. Play the tape, pausing it between each interview. These are real people talking at their natural speed so they can be difficult to understand during a first listening. The first time students listen, they should just concentrate on the first task (which is actually pretty easy!). This task focuses on the ingredients that are used in the three dishes.

Answers

recipe 1: all the ingredients listed except garlic and rice
recipe 2: all the ingredients listed except red pepper and beans
recipe 3: all the ingredients listed except cream and cheese

Transcript   3 minutes 15 seconds

The three recipes are recorded twice on the tape.

Recipe One.

TONY: Hi. My name is Tony, and I'm from China.

WOMAN: Tony, what's your favorite food?

TONY: Oh, I'm a big seafood lover, and the favorite dish is steamed flounder with ginger and scallions. I always start off with the freshest flounder I could buy. And I marinate it in soy sauce overnight. Then I place it in a steamer, and steam it for about three to four minutes. I chop up some fresh scallion and some julienned ginger slices, and place it on top of the fish, and let it steam for about another three to four minutes. On a separate pan, I take a little bit of vegetable oil, and heat it up. When the fish is ready to be taken out of the steamer, I pour the hot oil all over the fish with the ginger and scallion. Then I garnish it with a little parsley, and I serve it hot to my guests.

Recipe Two.

WANDA: Hi! My name is Wanda, and I'm from New York City, and my favorite dish is "Mama Pearl's double-seasoned fried chicken." You take some chicken pieces, and you wash them off, and . . . season them with garlic salt, garlic powder, thyme, oregano, and a little seasoned salt if you like. Then you put the chicken aside.

Take a brown paper bag, put it – fill it halfway with flour, and season it with the same seasoning that you seasoned your chicken with. Take the chicken pieces, put it inside the brown paper bag, close the top, hold it, and shake it so that the flour and the seasoning goes all the way through the chicken. Then you take a cast-iron skillet, and you fill it with peanut oil, and you make sure the oil is really, really hot. Don't let it smoke, but make sure it's hot because that's the secret. Then you take the chicken pieces, and you put it in the oil, and you turn it until it's golden brown, and when it's done, you take it out of the pot, and you place it on a brown paper bag. It's really important to drain the chicken on the brown paper bag – it does something to the flavor. But there you have it, and all you have to do is eat – it's delicious!

Recipe Three.

TREVOR: Hello, my name's Trevor, and I come from England. And my favorite dish is roast beef and Yorkshire pudding. Now everyone knows how to make roast beef, but not many people know how to make Yorkshire pudding. So I'm going to describe it for you. OK, first the ingredients: You take one cup of flour, half a teaspoon of salt, a half a cup of milk, half a cup of water, and two eggs. Now you beat all that together until it becomes smooth and h-has bubbles on the top. Then you melt a quarter cup of . . . of butter, and you place that in a baking pan. Then you add the rest of the ingredients to the baking pan, you put that in the oven for thirty minutes at three hundred and seventy-five degrees. Now after that it'll come out brown and crispy and golden, and you serve that with roast potatoes, roast beef, uh . . . vegetables, and some gravy – it's so delicious!

procedure continues on next page

2 Listen again

1. Have students concentrate on the methods of cooking. To make the task easier, the methods are summarized in three sets of simplified instructions.

2. Pause the tape after each speaker to give students time to write in their answers.

Answers

See the previous page for the transcript to this activity.

1. Tony is from **China**. 1. flounder   2. Steam   3. ginger   4. oil
2. Wanda is from **New York City**. 2. brown, bag   3. shake it   4. skillet
   5. Drain
3. Trevor is from **England**.   1. flour, salt, half a cup   2. Beat   3. Melt
   4. oven, 375

3 Join a partner

1. Form an even number of pairs so that students can easily combine into groups of four or five in the last activity.

2. Have students compare their answers. If they found the previous listening task difficult, play the tape again before they start discussing the questions.

3. Now it's time for students to react to the tape. Remind them that there is no correct or incorrect answer to each question.

4 Pair work

Students should choose a dish that's relatively easy to prepare. Go around helping with vocabulary and the spelling of tricky ingredients.

5 Join another pair

Students should work on fluency by swapping recipes and discussing which ones they'd like to try.

Follow-up activity

Brainstorm the names of some ingredients that are popular in your students' countries. Write the information on the board.

Sample answers

fruit	grapefruit, pineapple, orange, mango, guava
vegetables	beans, peas, carrots, onions, scallions
meat	beef, lamb, pork, chicken, ham, turkey
fish and seafood	salmon, tuna, shrimp, anchovies, trout
herbs and spices	parsley, thyme, oregano, basil, pepper, ginger, nutmeg

Writing activity

Give students the following directions for a writing task: *Write your favorite recipe*.

Encourage students to choose recipes that do not have complicated steps. Tell them to follow the models on page 9 of their texts (i.e., write the name of the dish, list the ingredients, and then give the instructions in a series of numbered steps).

Activity A

page 10

Vocabulary

lettuce   a green vegetable with large leaves, often used in salads
tortilla   a piece of flat bread, often made from cornmeal
anchovy   a small, salty fish
syrup   liquid made with sugar
tropical   typical of or belonging to the hottest parts of the world
papaya   a kind of tropical fruit
mango   a kind of tropical fruit (plural: **mangoes**)
hint   a very small amount
tip   money that you give to the waiter or waitress to thank them for their services
offer   a special price that is lower than usual

1 Pair work

1. So that Activity A2 will work, make sure there is an even number of pairs (including, if necessary, one or more groups of three).

2. If possible, arrange the chairs to represent tables in a restaurant to help create the appropriate atmosphere. Encourage students to hold their books like menus, as if they're deciding what to order. Point out the useful phrases given in the speech balloon. Demonstrate how they're used by giving some examples of what you might order.

3. Tell students to take some time and decide what they're going to order. You may have to help some students by explaining various items on the menu. Remind students that, as in real life, they don't have to know what everything is before they decide what they want to eat – usually people pick the things they know they'll like unless they're feeling particularly adventurous, which may be risky in an unfamiliar restaurant!

4. As you go around the class, play the role of waiter/waitress and explain any items on the menu that are puzzling to your students (the customers). Don't worry if some pairs fail to spot the special offer at the bottom of the menu, because their attention will be drawn to it in Activity A2.

2 Join another pair

1. Combine the pairs into groups of four (or five).

2. Point out the phrases in the speech balloon. Thrifty students will want to take advantage of the offer, which may mean they'll need to change their orders.

3. If there's time, go around taking orders for drinks (but not food) from your customers. Your role-playing will help to maintain the atmosphere and make it easier for students to imagine they're in a restaurant.

Vocabulary

cancellation   a reservation that someone no longer wants to use
local specialty   a delicious dish from a nearby area
spicy   strongly flavored with hot spices
today's special   a dish that is not on the menu and that is only available today
check   a piece of paper that tells you how much you have to pay

1 Pair work

1. Tell students that they will first come up with their own answers and then compare them to what's said on the tape. Students need to realize that their own ideas are just as good as the ones in the taped dialogues and that in real life there is more than one appropriate way to say something.

2. As a class, brainstorm ideas for the first picture. Ask students what they think the waiter is saying, and what they think the women are saying in reply. Allow time for students to offer plenty of ideas, so they understand that there are many ways of expressing similar ideas in any given situation.

3. Put the students into pairs for them to continue the activity. They should write on the first line below the picture so that the second line can be used in Activity B2. There are no right answers, but do go around the class offering advice and answering questions as necessary.

Sample answers

1. A table for two?
   Good evening, do you have a reservation?
   Welcome! Nice to see you again.
2. Are you ready to order?
   Would you like to see the menu?
3. What they're having looks good!
   Ooh, I like the look of that!
   That must be today's special. I'm going to get that.
4. Can you explain what this is, please?
   Does this dish come with . . . (a certain food)?
   I'll have the steak, please.
5. Is everything all right?
   Can I get you anything else?
   How is everything?
6. Excuse me, I'm not sure this is correct.
   I think there's a mistake on the bill.

2 Listen 📼

1. When everyone's ready, play the tape, which presents a sample conversation for each situation. Pause the tape between each conversation to allow time for students to write. Again, they should not be worried if their answers don't match the tape.

2. Play the tape again, pausing between each conversation. Ask students to notice what the *reply* to each opening question or statement was. Don't leave out this step, because it's important for students to know how to react to what people say to them.

Answers

1. Good evening, may I help you?
2. Would you like something to drink before you order?
3. I wonder what those people are having.
4. Could you tell us what this is, please?
5. Well, are you enjoying your meal?
6. Um . . . I think there's a mistake on the check.

Transcript   2 minutes

One.

WAITER: Good evening, may I help you?
WOMAN 1: Ah . . . Good evening. Ah . . . Do you have a table for two, please?
WAITER: Uh . . . Have you got a reservation?
WOMAN 2: Uh . . . No, we didn't think we needed to.
WAITER: Oh, that's all right. We have a cancellation, as a matter of fact.
WOMAN 2: Oh, good.
WAITER: Would you step this way, please?
WOMAN 1: Great. Thank you.

Two.

WAITER: Would you like something to drink before you order?
WOMAN 2: Oh, yes, please, I'd like a mineral water.
WOMAN 1: And I'd like an iced tea, please.
WAITER: A mineral water and an iced tea. Certainly.

Three.

WOMAN 1: I wonder what those people are having.
WOMAN 2: Who, those people over there?
WOMAN 1: Yeah, ooh, it looks delicious!
WOMAN 2: Let's ask the waiter then.
WOMAN 1: Mmm.

Four.

WOMAN 2: Could you tell us what this is, please?
WAITER: Oh, that's a local specialty – it's broiled chicken served with rice in a spicy sauce.
WOMAN 2: I see, thanks.
WOMAN 1: Oh, and one more thing. What are those people having?
WAITER: Over there? Uh . . . They're having today's special – it's Beef Rémoulade.

Five.

WAITER: Well, are you enjoying your meal?
WOMAN 1: Yes. Oh, it's delicious, thank you.
WOMAN 2: Mmm, very good. Thank you.
WAITER: Just let me know when you're ready to order your dessert.
WOMAN 1: Mmm. OK, thanks.

Six.

WOMAN 1: Um . . . I think there's a mistake on the check.
WAITER: Oh, really?
WOMAN 2: I think you've given us the wrong one.
WAITER: Did I? Let me . . . let me see. . . . Oh, I'm so sorry, you're quite right. This is for table thirteen.
WOMAN 1: I didn't think we'd eaten that much!
WAITER: I'm sure you didn't. I'll be back in a moment.

page 11   **Vocabulary**

> **typical**   characteristic; very common in a particular region
> **featuring**   including as special items

Procedure

1. Be sure to look at the two tasks (Task 2 on page C-2 and Task 13 on page C-8) before the lesson so that you can answer any questions that may arise.

2. Arrange the class into groups of three (or four). If you have a multicultural class, this is an excellent chance for them to exchange information about their native cuisine.

3. Circulate among the groups as they write their menus. If necessary, remind students that short and simple menus are better (and take up less class time).

4. The next part of the activity begins when the menus have been written: One person in the group looks at Task 2 and then goes to play the role of waiter or waitress for a *different* group. This person takes the menu *with them*. The original group members stay in place and look at Task 13. They are now the customers. They'll be shown a new menu by the waiter/waitress who has joined them from a different group. The new menu, with unfamiliar foods on it, should generate questions that the waiter/waitress will answer.

5. When all the orders have been taken, reassemble the class and ask if there are any questions.

6. If there's time, the students who were waiters/waitresses should change places with one of the customers from their original group. This customer then becomes a waiter/waitress for a different group (using the menu he or she helped to originally write).

Writing activity

Give students the following directions for a writing task:

Write a menu like the one on page 10 that includes your favorite dishes.

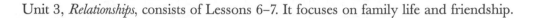

6 Families

Unit 3, *Relationships*, consists of Lessons 6–7. It focuses on family life and friendship.

page 12

Vocabulary

family tree   a diagram showing how the members of a family are related to each other
ex-husband   a woman's former husband, from whom she is now divorced
niece   the daughter of your brother or sister
nephew   the son of your brother or sister
great-grandmother   the mother of your grandmother
sister-in-law   the sister of your husband or wife, or your brother's wife
cousin   the child of your uncle and aunt
divorced   no longer legally married

1 Pair work

1. Have students form pairs (and one or more group of three if necessary). Note that depending on the language, various family relationships may have their own special names. For example, in English the same word, *uncle*, is used for the brother of one of your parents *and* for your aunt's husband (who isn't a blood relation, but is married to the sister of one of your parents). Other languages, however, might make a distinction between these two relationships by using two different words to describe them.

2. Allow students plenty of time to work through the four questions.

3. For the last part, make it clear that students should talk about James's relationship to everyone else in the family tree *and* their relationship to him. You may need to give some examples (see the answers that follow). Encourage students to make their descriptions as conversational as possible rather than following a set pattern (for example, "James and John are brothers." "James used to be married to Karen. He's her ex-husband." "Richard and Linda are James's parents. He's their son.")

Answers

Masculine equivalents of the words in the box at the top of page 12 of the Student's Book

grandfather	son	brother	husband	stepfather	nephew
father	grandson	brother-in-law	ex-husband	widower	cousin

Words that can be combined with *in-law*

daughter-in-law, son-in-law
sister-in-law, brother-in-law
mother-in-law, father-in-law

answers continue on next page

Activity A

page 12
continued

James's relationship to the people in the chart – and their relationship to him

James is Karen's ex-husband. (Karen is James's ex-wife.)
James is Nancy's husband. (Nancy is James's wife.)
James is Jennifer's brother. (Jennifer is James's sister.)
James is Steven's brother-in-law. (Steven is James's brother-in-law.)
James is John's brother. (John is James's brother.)
James is Lisa's brother-in-law. (Lisa is James's sister-in-law.)
James is Jessica's father. (Jessica is James's daughter.)
James is Jason's uncle. (Jason is James's nephew.)
James is Sarah's uncle. (Sarah is James's niece.)
James is Richard's son. (Richard is James's father.)
James is Linda's son. (Linda is James's mother.)
James is David's nephew. (David is Richard's uncle.)
James is Susan's nephew. (Susan is James's aunt.)
James is Robert's grandson. (Robert is James's grandfather.)
James is Mary's grandson. (Mary is James's grandmother.)

2 Work alone

Students who have no living relatives won't be able to do this. To spare them embarrassment it may be necessary to skip this section entirely, or if you think it's appropriate, you could pair them up with another student for this task.

3 Join a partner

1. Allow students time to explain to their partners why they like their favorite relatives.
2. Reassemble the class and look at the family tree again from Jason's perspective. Discuss how he is related to everyone else in the family. (Robert and Mary are his great-grandparents, David is his great-uncle, and so on.)

Activity B

page 13

Vocabulary

to associate   to connect ideas together

1 Work alone

1. It may be necessary to brainstorm a few suitable words with the whole class before students complete the task on their own (see the sample answers that follow).
2. While students are working, go around offering advice on suitable vocabulary. Encourage everyone to freely associate, and not just to make another list of relatives.

Sample answers

comfortable, warm, friendly, supportive, happy, close, love, security
strict, crowded, arguments, difficulties, tense

2 Group work

1. Point out the phrases in the speech balloons.

2. Students who come from different countries may have quite different family traditions, which would be interesting to discuss. If you have a multinational class, conclude the activity by having each group give a short report to the whole class on interesting points that they discussed.

Activity C

page 13

Pair work

1. Have each pair of students discuss the relationships between the people in the pictures. There may be more than one possible interpretation for each situation. For example, in the bottom left photo the younger woman (second from the left) isn't necessarily the little girl's mother: She might be her aunt (and the mother might be behind the camera, taking the photo) or she might be her stepmother. And if the younger man is her father, are the older couple his parents or his parents-in-law? Similar questions may be raised about the relationships of the people in the other photos.

2. After pairs have talked about the photos, reassemble the class and then ask a few pairs to tell the others what they decided about the relationships. Remind students again that there are no "right" answers, although certainly some relationships will be more likely than others.

Writing activity

Give students the following directions for a writing task:

Write about your family. Name each family member and tell how they are related to you. Give a brief description of each person (for example, their age and what they do). Think of one interesting thing to tell about each person.

Activity A	**1 Pair work**
page 14	

1. Have students form an even number of pairs for this activity so that they can easily combine into groups later. Don't spend too long on Activity A, or there won't be enough time for Activities B and C that follow.

2. Emphasize to students that there are no right or wrong answers to this task.

3. Make sure you allow students enough time to discuss various scenarios for the pictures before they join another pair. During the discussion period, go around the class answering questions about vocabulary.

2 Join another pair

Have pairs tell their stories to each other.

Activity B	**Vocabulary**
pages 15–16	

to get along with someone   to have a friendly relationship with someone
buddy   a close friend
to bond   to make a close relationship
hysterical   very funny
to click   to become friends very quickly
to wait an eternity   to wait for a very long time
to hit it off   to become friends very quickly
to be there for someone   to be ready to help someone
to gossip   to talk about other people's private lives
to have something in common   to share interests and attitudes
mirror   a reflection of yourself that shows your character
to rise to one's goals   to achieve what one wants in life
to take the blame for something   to say something is your fault
to hold a grudge   to feel anger, usually for a long time, toward someone you feel has treated you badly
to talk behind someone's back   to say bad things about someone when he or she is not present

1 Listen 📼

1. Review pertinent vocabulary items with students before the listening task, but don't try to explain all the words on the list. Students can complete the task without understanding all the new vocabulary; the list is here to assist you in answering questions afterwards.

2. Ask the students to review the chart so they know in advance what information they need to listen for. Tell them that they may hear more than one answer for some boxes in the chart, but they only need to write one answer to complete the task. Students who want to add more answers may do so.

3. Play the tape, pausing it where asterisks (***) appear in the transcript, so students have enough time to write their answers. You may want to have students compare notes with one another as well.

4. Although you should plan on playing the tape twice, have everyone try to note down answers in both columns the first time through.

5. Play the tape a third time, and ask students to note how the speakers first met their friends.

Answers

	Why they get along	What they do together
Tom's old friend Jeff	• share a lot of interests • like the same things • both funny	• something special • basketball game • camping
Tom's new friend Erica	• she's funny – makes him laugh	• go to the movies
Lori's old friend Steven	• share music in common	• go to see concerts • play in bands
Lori's new friend Mary	• have a lot in common (things they like to do, the way they live their lives) • both hard workers • both enjoy travel	• go to movies • go out for dinner • camping trip planned for the summer
Phyllis's old friend Dorothy	• been there for each other • she's a lot of fun	• sit around talking about old times • gossip about friends • talk about clothes, politics, etc.

Transcript   4 minutes 25 seconds

First, Tom.

INTERVIEWER: Who's your best friend?

TOM: Uh . . . My best friend is . . . uh . . . this guy . . . uh . . . Jeff Subick. He's . . . uh . . . he's been my friend for a long, long time. Old school . . . you know, school buddy.

INTERVIEWER: How did you meet?

TOM: Uh . . . We actually met very, very young in . . . uh . . . either kindergarten or first grade, like right from the beginning, you know, we were . . . we were friends.

INTERVIEWER: Why do you think you're such good friends?

transcript continues on next page

TOM: Uh . . . Well, we share a lot of interests, you know, . . . um . . . h-he and I, you know, like a lot of the same things. And . . . uh . . . I think he's funny, and I think he thinks I'm funny. I don't see him much anymore, uh . . . there's a lot of distance between us now. But I see him, like, two or three times a year, and when we do, we, you know, we try to do something special.

INTERVIEWER: Mm-hmm. Like what?

TOM: Uh . . . Well, we went to a . . . to a basketball game last year. Uh . . . We went camping for a week last summer. Um . . .

***

INTERVIEWER: Who's your newest friend?

TOM: I just . . . I just . . . uh . . . in my new job, I just met a girl, uh, this girl Erica, and she's . . . uh – Her and I hit it off right away so . . . and she's my newest friend.

INTERVIEWER: Mm-hmm. So you . . . uh – Where did you meet?

TOM: Yeah, . . . we met at the . . . at the job. We . . . uh . . . she got the . . . we both got . . . uh . . . trained the same day, and got, you know, the job together and kind of helped each other through the training process, and that kind of was how we, you know, bonded.

I like people who are funny, and she's just hysterical, and she was making me laugh all through the . . . you know, it's the . . . when I first met her she was making me laugh right away, and we just clicked, you know.

We s– we've been seeing a lot of each other lately. Um . . . We've been going to the movies and stuff, and . . . uh . . . um . . . we've been enjoying each other's company lately.

***

Now, Lori.

LORI: I'd say my oldest friend is . . . uh . . . Steven Jacobs. Uh . . . We've been friends, I guess, for . . . uh . . . well, a long time. Many years now.

INTERVIEWER: So how did you meet?

LORI: We were both in the percussion section of . . . uh . . . senior orchestra in high school. And . . . uh . . . when you're playing drums, you have a lot of rest time, so there was a lot of time to get to know each other and talk. And of course, we . . . uh . . . we shared music in common.

INTERVIEWER: So how often do you see each other, and do you get together?

LORI: Yeah, we . . . he lives in the city, too, and I'd say we see each other every couple of weeks. And still the love of music has . . . has . . . uh . . . has remained the major bond. We often go see concerts and . . . um . . . in fact, we've . . . uh . . . we've done a couple of things together . . . um . . . uh . . . you know, we've played together a couple of times in bands. Um . . . Yeah, he's a great guy.

***

INTERVIEWER: Who's your latest friend?

LORI: Oh, gosh, my newest friend is . . . uh . . . is a wonderful woman that I met at the theater on line for the ladies' room. We were waiting an eternity, and we started to talk, and we both loved what we were seeing. And . . . uh . . . we just really hit it off, and we went out for coffee after the performance.

We've gone to the movies several times. Uh . . . We've gone . . . we've gone out for dinner. Uh . . . We're planning to take a camping trip this summer together.

We seem to have a lot in common, uh . . . the things we like to do and the way we . . . uh . . . the way we live our lives. We're both . . . um . . . we're both hard workers, but we also like to travel, and we just seem to really hit it off.

***

Finally, Phyllis.

PHYLLIS: My oldest friend is Dorothy.

INTERVIEWER: And how did you and Dorothy meet?

PHYLLIS: Well, I met Dorothy, we were about eighteen years old, and she had come to New York, and she was evicted from her apartment. She couldn't pay the rent, and so I said, "Well, why don't you move in with me?" I had an apartment with an extra room, and that's how we met. We've been friends since then. She's been there for me, and I've been there for her, and she's just a lot of fun.

INTERVIEWER: What kinds of things do you do when you're together?

PHYLLIS: Well, we sit around, we talk about old times, we gossip about a lot of friends that we have in common. Uh . . . She's a wonderful storyteller, and so I love to hear her stories, and she's a fashion designer, so we talk about clothes and politics and a lot of things. We have a lot in common.

2 Group work

1. Have students look at the speech balloon to start off their discussions. The questions can be discussed in any order.

2. Circulate around the class. Encourage students to move on to the next question if their conversations bog down.

3 Listen 📼

Play the tape a couple of times, pausing between each interview. Again, students don't need to write down all the answers given here.

Answers

Tom
    You don't feel alone.
    You have people to share things with.

Lori
    Friends are a great mirror (you get to see yourself in a certain way).
    A good friend can help you rise to your goals.
    It's fun to have someone to share with.
    It's fun to have someone to do things you like to do.

Phyllis
    They're very supportive.
    They're there when you need them.

Transcript   1 minute 15 seconds

First, Tom.

INTERVIEWER: Why are friends important to you?

TOM: Well, friends are important because . . . um . . . you know, y-you don't feel alone if you have somebody who's a friend, or, you know, somebody close to you if you have people to share things with.

Now, Lori.

LORI: I'd say friends are . . . uh . . . friends are a great mirror: You get to see . . . um . . . you get to see yourself in a certain way. Um . . . If it's a good friend, he can . . . he can . . . help you . . . uh . . . help you rise to your goals and . . . uh – It's also just fun to have someone to share with, and . . . and . . . someone to do things that you like to do.

transcript continues on next page

Finally, Phyllis.

PHYLLIS: Oh, friends, well, I can't imagine
being without friends. They're very
supportive, they're . . . they're there when
you need them – a good friend always is,
and I like to help my friends, and I . . . I
do things for them, and we just share.

4 Join a partner

Encourage students to explain their own attitudes about friendship, and not just say
things such as "I agree with Tom" or "Me too," when discussing the question.

5 Group work

Explain that this activity is designed to get students to explore the limits of
friendship, perhaps comparing it implicitly with family relationships. There may be
some items on the list that students wouldn't expect anyone to do for them – not
even their parents.

Sample answers

Things that real friends do for each other:
wait for you if you're late
help you with your work
let you borrow their car or bike
never get angry with you
stand up for you in an argument
give you a lift to another city in their car

Communication task

Vocabulary

ballroom dancing   dancing together following fixed steps, such as tango or waltz steps
motto   a short sentence that expresses a rule for good behavior (plural: **mottoes**)
hang gliding   flying in a very small aircraft that does not have an engine
bungee jumping   jumping off a high place, such as a bridge, with your feet attached
   to a long elastic rope that pulls you back before your head hits the ground
Rollerblading   moving around on special shoes that have small wheels on the
   bottoms
Look before you leap.   Before you do something risky, make sure you think about
   what problems your actions may create.

Procedure

1. Be sure to look at the two tasks (Task 3 on page C-3 and Task 14 on page C-9)
   before the lesson so that you can answer any questions that may arise. Students
   will be exchanging information about the people in their books.

2. Encourage students not to simply read out the information verbatim, but to try to describe the people naturally. You may need to demonstrate this (for example, "Let me tell you about Scott Simmons. He's 32 years old and he's a lawyer. He likes reading and he also likes to cook . . .").

3. Have students take turns describing the three people in their book. Students who are listening should decide who sounds most like a potential friend and explain why.

4. Reassemble the class and find out which of the six people was the most popular. Look at the six mottoes – does everyone understand them? Do any members of the class have a motto of their own? Do you? Have a class discussion about mottoes.

Writing activity

Give students the following directions for a writing task:

Write about your best friend. Describe him or her and explain how you first met. Tell why you get along well with each other.

Review puzzles

page 17

See page xii of the Introduction for notes on puzzles.

The vocabulary in Puzzle A is from Lessons 1–3. The vocabulary in Puzzle B is from Lessons 4–7.

Puzzle A

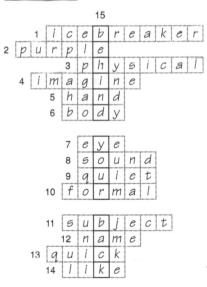

Puzzle B

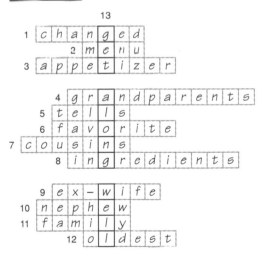

8 Nine to five

Unit 4, *Earning a living*, consists of Lessons 8–9. It focuses on the advantages and disadvantages of different kinds of jobs.

Activity A

page 18

Vocabulary

role   a position (in a company)

salary and benefits   the money you are paid for doing a job and the other advantages of working, such as health insurance and payments when you are sick or when you retire

Other important vocabulary includes all the words listed in Activity A2.

1 Pair work

1. Give everyone enough time to think of several advantages and disadvantages of each job. (In Activity B they'll hear some more about two of the jobs illustrated.) The expressions in the speech balloon will help students to organize their discussion.

2. Ask a few students to tell the rest of the class what they'd like most/least about each job and why.

2 Pair work

1. Have students look at the three examples to make sure they understand what they have to do.

2. If your students have highlighters, have them highlight the words they don't know instead of putting a circle around them. If students want to review new vocabulary, they can more easily locate highlighted text.

3. When they've finished, check the answers with the whole class and answer any questions students may have.

Answers

People's roles at work	Salary and benefits	Job types
boss supervisor employer manager employee	pay retirement plan health insurance raise hourly wages overtime pay	full-time job freelance position office worker part-time job temporary position

Vocabulary

duty   a task you have to do as part of your work
to stay on top of   to keep up with; not to be too slow and fall behind
incoming call   a phone call that is made to your office
partner   a member of a firm of lawyers or accountants
to log (in)   to keep a record of
to route   to send to the right place
to flip a switch   to press a switch to turn something on
to plunge   to push
pulp   the parts of the fruit that are left over after the juice has been taken out
shift   the hours that you work
cool   excellent; very good; nice
jumpy   nervous

1 Listen 📼

1. Before students listen, remind them that there's no need to understand every word. Have them look at the pictures and see if they can figure out what each one shows.

2. Play the tape, pausing it between the two conversations. Have students check the duties they hear described on the tape.

3. Play the tape again if necessary.

Answers

Phil: Pictures checked should be the second (incoming calls), third (handling faxes), and fifth (greeting people).
Working hours: 9 to 5

Christopher: Pictures checked should be the first (making juice), third (washing the fruits and vegetables), and fifth (keeping the counter clean).
Working hours: 10 to 6

Transcript   2 minutes 30 seconds

First, Phil.

BOSS: OK. Well, it's a very busy office, so let me tell you right away: The phone is going to ring all day! You really have to stay on top of the incoming calls. And then of course take a message for every call.

PHIL: OK.

BOSS: Um . . . Of course when people come in, you have to greet them, seat them, and direct them where to go when the partner is ready to see them.

PHIL: Mm-hmm.

BOSS: Um . . . The fax machine is right behind your desk here, as you can – Oh, here's comes a fax now. OK, when the faxes come in, you have to log them in, and make sure they get routed to the appropriate office.

PHIL: Right.

BOSS: Also, partners will leave faxes for you to send through the machine as well. You have to make sure that they were received on the other end.

PHIL: OK.

BOSS: Uh . . . Hours are nine to five, of course. (Mm-hmm.) You can take an hour for lunch anywhere between twelve and two, any time that you like.

PHIL: Oh, good.

BOSS: That's about it.

transcript continues on next page

Activity B

*page 19
continued*

Now, Christopher.

BOSS: It's really pretty simple. Basically, you make sure that all the fruits and vegetables are washed, (Hmm.) and you put them in separate compartments. And when people come to the counter, they'll tell you what combinations they want –

CHRISTOPHER: Separate compartments in the refrigerator?

BOSS: In the refrigerator, (OK.) right. Because everything should be cold so (OK.) that you don't have to add ice to the juice. And the juicer's very simple: You just flip the switch in the back, and you plunge the vegetables through the top, and the juice comes out. And after each juice that you make, you must clean the juicer, it's very important, so that –

CHRISTOPHER: Does that mean like take the pulp out and . . . ?

BOSS: Take the basket out, take the pulp out, . . .

CHRISTOPHER: Oh, the whole thing.

BOSS: . . . rinse it out, (OK.) and put it back together. Um . . . Let's see, this job is from ten to six, and you get an hour lunch break. You can have something from the juice bar if you like. (Oh, good.) We . . . we kind of ask you to stay in the area in case we need you because sometimes it does get busy, and we have to cut down your shift, (Sure.) your lunch hour, rather. Um . . . Let's see, is there anything else? Oh, yeah, keep the counter clean because that's what everyone always sees!

CHRISTOPHER: Great!

BOSS: So I think you're ready to start.

CHRISTOPHER: I feel ready to start.

BOSS: Good.

2 Join a partner

Play the tape again if there is any disagreement about the correct answers.

3 Listen 🔲

Play the tape, pausing between each conversation to give the students time to write their answers. You may need to play the tape twice.

Answers

Phil	Christopher
boss was supportive and nice coworkers were very nice and welcomed him	not very complicated pleasant boss people are really friendly efficient, enjoyable place to work

Transcript   1 minute 40 seconds

First, Phil.

FRIEND: Hey, Phil. How was your day?

PHIL: Oh, actually, I had a great day. Today was my first day at the new job. And I thought it was going to be kind of a dull place, but it's very exciting, it's a great company to work for.

FRIEND: What was your favorite part of the day?

PHIL: Well, I was very surprised that my boss was . . . um . . . a very supportive and . . . and nice person, and in fact all the coworkers there seemed to be . . . um . . . very nice to me, and they welcomed me.

FRIEND: Oh, that's great. Are you looking forward to going back tomorrow?

PHIL: Yes, I am. As a matter of fact, uh . . . I'm actually working quite late tomorrow. They said on some days I would be . . . um . . . spending a little bit more time there, so I'll make a little bit more money.

Now, Christopher.

FRIEND: Hey, how was your first day on the job?

CHRISTOPHER: Y-you know, uh, it was . . . it was really fun. I mean, I was looking forward to the job and everything. It's a good job, but I didn't think it would be as enjoyable as it was.

FRIEND: Oh, really? (Yeah.) How was it, like . . . ?

CHRISTOPHER: Well, I mean, I went in this morning, and . . . and I met my new boss. And she was really cool, and she laid out everything I needed to do, and . . . it's really not very complicated. And it's . . . it's fun, and she's a very pleasant woman.

FRIEND: So you're looking forward to staying with this job?

CHRISTOPHER: I am. I mean, if it's any . . . if today was any indication of what's going to happen, then, yeah, I'm very happy, because the people are really friendly. Even at lunch break . . . even at the lunch hour when it was really crowded, people stayed relaxed and cool and didn't get angry and didn't get jumpy, and it's a very efficient, enjoyable place to work.

FRIEND: Sounds fun.

4 Join a partner

Play the tape again if there is any disagreement about the correct answers.

Activity C

page 19

Vocabulary

ideal   perfect
goal   aim or purpose; ambition

Group work

1. Arrange students into groups of three or four. Remind them that the speech balloons offer some suggested ways of starting their conversations.

2. After the groups have had sufficient time to discuss the questions, reassemble the class and have various students tell the others about their ideal jobs. Ask the students if they have any questions about the vocabulary.

3. Before the next class, ask students to read the article on page 20 of the Student's Book and guess the missing words.

Writing activity

Give students the following directions for a writing task:

If you have a job, write a description of what you do on a typical day. If you don't have a job, write a description of a typical day at school or college.

9 An interesting job

Vocabulary

sound track   the sounds and music of a film
celery   a vegetable with long white and green stems
iron   an appliance used to take the wrinkles out of clothes
hoof   a horse's foot (plural: **hooves**)
coconut   a large fruit, with a hard, brown shell; from the cocoa palm tree
toilet plunger   a rubber device with a wooden handle, used to clear a blocked toilet
to scrape   to make an unpleasant noise by moving an object across a rough surface
ax   a tool used for cutting trees
concrete   a mixture of cement, sand, and water used to make buildings
to punch   to hit with your fist
appreciation   recognition of someone's work
artistic   creative

1 Read/listen

1. Ask your students to read the article, and guess the missing words before coming to class. If it is not possible to assign the reading for homework, allow plenty of class time for students to complete the task.

2. Play the tape.

3. Have students highlight any vocabulary in the passage they would like to remember.

Transcript and answers   2 minutes 10 seconds
Missing words are in bold type.

Walking for a Living

A Foley artist earns a living adding sounds like footsteps to movie sound tracks. Footsteps are added in sound studios because when a movie is filmed, the **microphones** are aimed at the actors' mouths, not their **feet** – and because real footsteps just don't sound natural.

A Foley artist watches a **movie** in the sound studio and follows the actor's footsteps on a special stage, keeping time with the **actor's** movements. The Foley artist wears the same kind of shoes that the actor wore and walks on the same surface. For example, if the actor wore boots and **walked** on a wood floor, the Foley artist does, too. A skilled Foley artist can match the footsteps exactly to the character the actor is playing and even show **emotions** like fear or surprise.

Foley artists also add all kinds of sound effects to movies. In a horror film, the sound of **bones** breaking is made by snapping celery and dry spaghetti. The sound of burning bodies is created by dripping water onto a hot iron. The sound of horses' hooves used to be made using **coconuts**, but modern Foley artists prefer to use a toilet plunger. The sound of **ice-skating** is made by scraping an ax across concrete – real ice doesn't sound natural enough.

Jack Foley invented this way of adding **sound effects** to movies in the 1930s.

Before that, moviemakers used recordings of sound effects and added them to the movie sound track. Now Foley artists work on almost every movie. The **noises** you hear when someone is punched and falls are created by a Foley artist – actors only **pretend** to hit each other, and their "injuries" are created by makeup artists.

Most Foley artists are very private people. Their work is done in special sound studios, and they don't appear in front of the public or even in front of the **camera**. And they don't get the appreciation they deserve – if they do the job right, the **audience** doesn't even notice.

2 Join a partner

1. Decide whether you want this to be a written or a discussion activity.
2. Go over the answers with the whole class.

Answers

1. The artist adds sound effects to the movie sound track.
2. Microphones are directed at actors' mouths, not their feet – and real footsteps don't sound realistic.
3. The artist can match the footsteps exactly to the character and show emotions like fear or surprise.
4. By scraping an ax across concrete.
5. They're named after Jack Foley, who invented this way of adding sound effects to movies.
6. They don't get much appreciation. If they do the job well, their work isn't even noticed because they don't appear in public or in front of the camera.

Activity B

page 21

Vocabulary

stunt   an exciting trick that looks dangerous
makeup   colored substances used on your face to improve or change your appearance
lens   the glass "eye" that records the images on the film inside a camera
to splice   to join together (pieces of film)

1 Pair work

Encourage students to speculate on what they think the various people do on a daily basis in their jobs. Don't give students any help here, as they will be exposed to more detailed job descriptions in the next activity.

Answers

top row:	makeup artist	stuntperson
middle row:	animal trainer	cameraperson
bottom row:	grip	film editor

Activity B

page 21
continued

2 Communication task

Procedure

1. Be sure to look at the three tasks (Task 4 on page C-3, Task 11 on page C-7, and Task 15 on page C-9) before the lesson so you can answer any questions that may arise. Students will be exchanging information about the jobs in their books.

2. Encourage students to paraphrase the information given in the description, rather than read it aloud word for word. You may want them to read the descriptions and then cover them up while they tell their partners about the two jobs. A speech balloon accompanies each task, providing students with a good model for starting a description.

3. After hearing the job descriptions, the other students should be able to guess which job is being described. If students are not sure which job is being described, tell them to ask questions to find out more information.

Activity C

page 21

Vocabulary

nine-to-five job   a typical office job with fixed hours
unpredictable   not able to be judged or decided in advance

Group work

1. Arrange the class into groups of three or four for them to discuss the questions.

2. To conclude the activity, ask each group to summarize its answers to the last two questions for the rest of the class.

Writing activity

Give students the following directions for a writing task:

Write a description of your ideal job or the job you want to have when you finish your education.

10 Useful things

Unit 5, *Modern inventions*, consists of Lessons 10–11. It focuses on how gadgets and inventions work and how useful they are.

Activity A

pages 22–23

Vocabulary

invention   a machine or system that has never been designed or made before
special occasion   an event that you want to remember, such as a birthday or anniversary
VCR   videocassette recorder
to duplicate   to copy
influence   effect (on one's life)

1 Pair work

1. Arrange students into an even number of pairs so that the pairs can easily combine into groups for Activity A3.

2. Don't spend too much time on this vocabulary activity. The more interesting discussion ideas are in the activities on page 23.

3. Make sure everyone has matched the labels and pictures correctly. Answer any questions students may have.

Answers

Clockwise from top right: 3, 2, 6, 8, 4, 1, 7, 5

2 Pair work

Tell students that process of elimination will solve most of the trickier items, so if they are confused by a particular definition, they should move on and come back to it later.

Answers

3 (microwave oven)	4 (camcorder)
6 (mouse)	1 (remote control)
8 (fax machine)	– cassette recorder (cassette player)
– dishwasher	5 (photocopier)
2 (answering machine)	7 (clock radio)

3 Join another pair

1. Combine the pairs.

2. Go through the phrases in the speech balloon with the class before they begin the discussion. The grammar of some of the phrases is rather complex, but even conditionals should be quite easy for students to use if they stick to the example sentences and complete the sentences with infinitives. Give some examples about one of the items that you think is particularly useful.

Activity B Group work

page 23

1. Demonstrate how to do the activity by explaining how to use something. For example, your classroom cassette player (which is probably more complicated to operate than students realize): "This is how you use this cassette player. First, you put the plug into the electrical outlet. Next, you put a cassette into this slot here. Make sure the cassette is the right way up. Then you . . ."

2. While the groups are doing this activity, go around offering help and advice. This is a very open-ended activity and quite challenging, so be prepared to help with vocabulary.

Activity C Vocabulary

page 23

riddle   a type of question that describes something in an unexpected way and has an amusing answer

ceiling   the top part of the inside of a room

gadget   a small device or machine (such as a can opener)

Group work

1. Have students work in groups to guess what the riddle describes. (It's a table.) They may have some other imaginative answers that fit part of the definition, but not all of it (for example, a ladder, a bookcase, a tree, a bed, a bench).

2. Tell students to work alone for a few moments thinking of an object and writing a riddle for it. You may need to give them a few ideas to start off. Here are other versatile objects that you could suggest: rug, ruler, tennis racket, baseball bat, toothpick, pencil, sheet of paper, coin, necktie, shoelace, brown paper bag.

3. Students should take turns reading their riddles aloud to the rest of their group. Each student should read his or her entire riddle before group members start to guess.

4. Reassemble the class. Ask each group to try one of their best riddles on the entire class to see if they can guess the answer.

Before the next lesson

page 23

Make sure that everyone notices the instructions on the bottom of page 23. Students will need to bring gadgets to class in order to successfully do Activity C in the next lesson. The gadget need not be high-tech: It can be something quite simple like a fountain pen, a pencil sharpener, or a pocket calculator. Watches are good – there are so many different kinds, many of which are quite difficult to operate.

11 Great ideas?

Activity A

page 24

Vocabulary

product   something you can buy
on sale   available at a cheaper price than normal
artificial   not natural
burglar   a person who steals things from people's homes
range   the maximum distance at which something works
furniture cushion   a pillow that you put on a chair or sofa to make it more comfortable
disappointed   unhappy because something is not as good as you had hoped

1 Pair work

Tell students this activity will help to prepare them for the listening activity that follows.

2 Listen 📼

1. Play the tape, pausing between each of the three passages. The three products described in this activity *are* all real products (although Safe-T-Man doesn't come with two sets of clothes – the purchaser has to supply the clothes).

2. Make it clear to students that they don't need to understand every word to complete the chart. Since the speakers are talking quite fast, the students will need to hear the tape at least twice to get all of the information.

3. Remind your students that they only need to write one feature for each item (although more are listed here).

Answers

Product	Function	One important feature	Price
1. Pencorder	records short messages and works like a pen	records up to 20 seconds of messages	on sale today for $39.95 (usually $49.95)
2. Safe-T-Man	keeps you safe (by making people think you are not alone)	weighs less than 10 pounds/5 kilograms available in 3 styles comes with 2 sets of clothes	$99.95
3. TV Remote Control Locator	helps you find your remote control	75-foot/25-meter range works through walls, windows, and furniture cushions	$24.95

see next page for transcript

Transcript   4 minutes 35 seconds

One. Pencorder.

STAN: Thank you. And welcome to "Great Ideas," the show where we find out about some really incredible products. First, let's say hello to our old friend, Bob Landon. Hi, Bob.

BOB: Hi, Stan.

STAN: Hey, that's a nice pen you've got there.

BOB: Yes, it is, isn't it? But it's not just a pen. It's a Pencorder.

STAN: A what?

BOB: A Pencorder. It's a pen and a tape recorder. Here, let me show you. I'm going to press this red button at the top of the pen. (Uh-huh.) Now you tell us the telephone number that viewers have to call to order a product from "Great Ideas."

STAN: Sure – it's 1-800-555-1234.

BOB: OK, now listen.

STAN: Sure – it's 1-800-555-1234. Wow, it recorded my voice!

BOB: Right. Now every time I have to remember a phone number, or an address, I just record it on my Pencorder. (Oh.) It records up to twenty seconds of messages. And if I want to write something down, the Pencorder also works as a pen.

STAN: What a *great idea*! Just one more question, Bob. How much *is* the Pencorder?

BOB: Well, usually the Pencorder is forty-nine ninety-five. (Ooh.) Today, it's on sale for only thirty-nine ninety-five.

STAN: That's incredible!

Two. Safe-T-Man.

STAN: Thank you. Thank you. And now, he-e-e-e-re's Melissa! Hi, Melissa. Do you have another *great idea* for us?

MELISSA: Yes, I do, Stan.

STAN: Good! But first of all, can you tell me: Who's that guy sitting by the window?

MELISSA: Oh, he's my Safe-T-Man.

STAN: Your safety man?

MELISSA: Safe-T-Man. He may look human, but he's not. He's an artificial man. He weighs less than ten pounds.

STAN: Hmm. What does he do?

MELISSA: He sits there and keeps me safe. You know, I live alone, and my neighborhood isn't very safe.

STAN: Yeah.

MELISSA: Well, burglars will go away when they see my Safe-T-Man sitting by the window. (Ah.) They'll think that someone is with me. When I'm home alone, I'll feel safe.

STAN: That certainly is a *great idea*.

MELISSA: He's available in three styles: light skin with blond hair, light skin with gray hair, and dark skin with dark hair.

STAN: Fantastic!

MELISSA: And he comes with two sets of clothes. (Oh.) A jogging suit and a business suit.

STAN: So tell us, Melissa. How much is this amazing product?

MELISSA: Well, you can get Safe-T-Man for just ninety-nine ninety-five by calling the number that is on your television screen now.

STAN: That's an incredibly low price for such a *great idea*, Melissa.

MELISSA: It sure is.

Three. TV Remote Control Locator.

STAN: Thank you very much. Ooh, now it's time to watch my favorite show on TV. But . . . oh, no, I can't find the remote control.

BOB: You need some help, Stan?

STAN: Oh, hi, Bob. You can help me find the remote control?

BOB: Well, I can't. But the TV Remote Control Locator can. It finds your remote control for you.

STAN: Oh, it does?

BOB: Yeah. Press that red button on the TV.

STAN: OK. Here goes!

BOB: Hear that sound?

STAN: Yes, it's coming from under the couch.

BOB: Take a look.

STAN: Oh, yeah, here's the remote control. Thanks, Bob.

BOB: Don't thank me. Thank the TV Remote Control Locator.

STAN: Ha! What a great idea! I'm always losing my remote control.

BOB: Well, not anymore. The TV Remote Control Locator has a seventy-five-foot range, and it works through walls, windows, and furniture cushions.

STAN: That's amazing. What does it cost?

BOB: The TV Remote Control Locator is only twenty-four ninety-five. That's right. Only twenty-four ninety-five.

STAN: Well, that sure is a *great idea*, isn't it, folks? Thanks a lot, Bob.

3 Join a partner

1. Have students compare the information in their charts. Make sure they understand that the information in their charts may not be exactly the same. Circulate around the class to see if students are in general agreement about the answers. You may need to play the tape one more time to settle any disagreements.

2. Draw students' attention to the phrases in the speech balloon, which will help them to answer the discussion questions.

Activity B

page 25

Vocabulary

inventor   a person who designs or creates something new

sales license   a contract that allows a company to sell a product

design   the way something looks and how well it works

native   related to the place where you were born

plant seed   a small part of a plant from which a new plant will grow

microscope   a machine that makes very small things look bigger so that you can study them

hook   a curved device for catching or holding something (such as the hook at the end of a fishing line)

attached   joined together

fabric   material; cloth

streetcar   a vehicle that travels on special rails that are set into city streets (a tram)

mechanical   operated by a machine, not by hand

sketchbook   a book in which you make rough drawings

inspired   feeling moved to create something or do something difficult

significant   having a strong or important effect (on something)

see next page for procedure

1 Read/listen

1. Have students work in pairs or alone, reading the article and trying to guess the missing words. Tell students that it's OK if they can't guess some of the words since they will hear the words when they listen to the tape.

2. Play the tape, pausing between the information about each inventor to give students time to work. Ask students if they have any questions about "wrong guesses" they may have made, and help them decide which of their words, although not on the tape, are plausible answers.

3. Have students, alone or in pairs, do the comprehension questions and check their answers with you.

Transcript and answers   2 minutes

Missing words are in bold type.

Yoshiro Nakamats

Dr. Yoshiro Nakamats **patented** the first floppy disk in 1950. Nakamats, an **inventor** at Tokyo University in Japan, holds twenty-three hundred other patents, including one for **golf** club designs. IBM, a computer company, bought the sales license for the disks. They **improved** Nakamats' design and started selling floppy disks in 1970.

Georges de Mestral

One day in the 1950s Georges de Mestral was **walking** in his native Switzerland, when he noticed some **plant** seeds sticking to his jacket. He looked at them under a microscope and saw that the **seeds** were covered with tiny hooks, which **attached** themselves to the fabric of his clothing. This gave him the idea for Velcro™. The first Velcro™ was made by **hand** in France and

took a long time to make. Today **astronauts** use Velcro™ to prevent objects from **moving** around when they are traveling in space.

Mary Anderson

The windshield wiper was invented in 1903 by Mary Anderson, a woman from Alabama, U.S.A. While Anderson was riding a **streetcar** during a trip to New York City, she noticed that the driver often had to get out to wipe **snow** from the windshield. She quickly drew an idea for a **mechanical** windshield wiper in her sketchbook. Later she tried to sell her **idea** to a Canadian company, but the company decided that the invention wouldn't be **successful**. Anderson gave up on trying to sell her **invention** and never made any money from it.

Answers

Which inventor . . . ?

1. Mary Anderson
2. Yoshiro Nakamats
3. Georges de Mestral

4. Mary Anderson
5. Yoshiro Nakamats

2 Join a partner

Students should compare their answers and discuss which of the inventions they think was the most important.

Activity C

page 25

Group work

1. Have students form groups of three or four and take turns describing their gadgets. Remind students that the bags must remain closed until everyone has had a chance to make their guesses.

2. If students have forgotten to bring a gadget to class, this activity should be done in the next class.

Activity D

page 25

Communication task

Vocabulary

flashlight   a small, handheld light powered by batteries
emergency   an unexpected, dangerous situation
candle   a stick made of wax that is burned to give off light
battery   a small container in which electricity is stored
straw   a hollow tube you use to drink through
chlorine   a chemical that is used to purify drinking water
filter   a screen that cleans whatever passes through it
replacement filter   a new filter that you use when the old one is worn out
inversion   turning upside down
ankle   the part of your body between your leg and your foot
adjustable strap   a band of material that can be made smaller or larger to fit
instructional video   a video that explains how to use something

Procedure

1. Be sure to look at the three tasks (Task 5 on page C-4, Task 10 on page C-7, and Task 16 on page C-10) before the lesson so you can answer any questions that may arise.

2. Arrange the class into groups of three or four (in a group of four, two students can look together at one of the tasks). Each student has pictures of all three inventions and a detailed description of one of them. The idea is for students to ask one another questions to find out more about each invention.

3. Allow groups a few moments to read their descriptions through (and if necessary, ask you questions) before the group members begin asking one another questions.

4. To conclude the activity, ask students to decide which invention they think is the most useful and which they think is the least useful.

Writing activity

Give students the following directions for a writing task:

Write a paragraph about the gadget that you brought to class for Activity C.

12 Threats to our environment

Unit 6, *The environment*, consists of Lessons 12–13. It focuses on some of the problems facing the environment and ways of reducing the effects of those problems.

Activity A
page 26

Vocabulary

the environment   the air, water, and land around us
damage   harm or destruction
to deplete   to reduce the amount of something
ozone layer   a layer of air, high above the earth, that contains a special kind of oxygen
radiation   rays from the sun that cause skin cancer

1 Pair work

1. Before starting the first activity, skim *both* Lessons 12 and 13 before class. In presenting this topic, every effort has been made to avoid cultural imperialism, or to impose "liberal" Western values on other cultures. Still, it's possible that the text may be perceived as doing just this. Therefore, in teaching this lesson, allow students as many opportunities as possible to put their own views forward, and make sure that they don't feel that their nation is being criticized. Although thought-provoking, this unit isn't intended to be depressing or "heavy."

2. Begin the activity by going over the words in the vocabulary box to the left of the three pictures.

3. Arrange students into an even number of pairs so that the pairs can easily combine for Activity A2. Allow them enough time to compose their descriptions.

4. Ask one pair to describe one of the photos, and then ask other pairs to say more about it. Ask different pairs to do the same with the other two photos. You may want to ask students to suggest additional words that can be used to talk about the pictures.

2 Join another pair

1. Have pairs combine to form small groups to discuss the questions.

2. To conclude the activity, find out from students in each group which problem(s) they consider to be most serious.

Activity B
page 27

Vocabulary

illegal   against the law
ivory   the hard, white, smooth substance that an elephant's tusks are made of
jewelry   decorative objects you wear, such as necklaces or bracelets
tusk   a very long tooth of an elephant
profitable   resulting in a profit; money-making
hunting   killing animals for food or sport
compensation   money that is paid by someone responsible for damage or inconvenience

stable staying at the same level
conservationist a person who wants to protect animals and plants
sensitive having deep feelings or understanding
medicinal drug a drug that is used to treat illnesses
cure something that makes a sick person healthy again
profit the amount of money made from a business

1 Read/listen 📼

1. Have students read the left-hand column of the article ("The African Elephant") and guess what the missing words might be. They may work alone or in pairs.

2. Play "The African Elephant" part of the tape (but not the "What do you think?" questions) so that students can check their work and fill in the blanks with the words that they couldn't guess.

3. Put students into pairs (if they aren't already) and play the "What do you think?" questions. Have each pair discuss the questions.

4. Repeat this same procedure with the right-hand column of the article ("Medicinal Plants").

5. Another option: Have everyone do Activity B1 individually (writing out their answers to the "What do you think?" questions) and then form groups for Activity B2.

Transcript and answers 3 minutes 35 seconds

Missing words are in bold type.

The African Elephant

In 1990, over one hundred countries signed an international agreement to make it **illegal** to buy or sell ivory, which is mainly used for jewelry. Most ivory is made from the tusks of African **elephants**. These tusks are very valuable – one pair is worth more than three times what an African **farmer** or factory worker earns in a year.

Hunting elephants was so profitable that from 1979 to 1989 the number of elephants in **Africa** fell from one point three million to six hundred thousand. It was feared that by the year 2000 there would be none left. However, since 1990 there has been much less illegal **hunting**, thanks to the international agreement.

But it costs a lot of money to preserve elephants. Game wardens must be hired to **protect** them, land must be set aside for them, and when they destroy a farmer's crops, the farmer must be paid compensation.

Zimbabwe and four other African countries say that some of the elephants should be **killed** legally. This would help keep the population stable, and selling the ivory would help pay for preserving the elephants. But **conservationists** say that making ivory legal to sell would lead to even more illegal hunting. Others say that it is wrong to kill elephants because they are sensitive animals who feel emotional **pain** at the death of other elephants.

What do you think?
• Should the sale of ivory be made legal again?
• Is it right to kill some elephants to save others?
• Should a group of countries be allowed to tell another country what it should do?

transcript continues on next page

Activity B

*page 27
continued*

Medicinal Plants

When settlers in the United States spread west in the 1800s, they thought nothing of cutting down **forests** and killing wildlife to develop their country.

Today, developing countries are cutting down their forests because their people want a better life. But **scientists** say that this is a disaster. The rain forests are home to half the world's species. Undiscovered rain-forest plants could be used as **medicinal** drugs to treat diseases like AIDS and cancer. Two of today's most powerful anti-cancer medicines come from a single rain-forest **flower**. Many kinds of plants, which could be the sources of tomorrow's cures, are being destroyed at the rate of fifty to one hundred every day.

Developing countries think that it is wrong for people who **destroyed** their own forests long ago to tell them not to develop. They also feel that when a drug company discovers a **cure** in their rain forest, the company should share its profits with them.

What do you think?
- Should developing countries have the right to cut down their forests, as the United States did?
- Now that we know the rain forest is an important resource, does the world have the right to tell individual countries what to do with their rain forests?
- Should a drug company share its profits with a developing country when it uses a rain-forest plant as a medicine – even if the country did nothing to research, develop, and market the drug?

2 Group work

Have students compare their answers. If the students were in pairs for Activity B1, separate them into different groups so that each group consists of three or four students, all from different pairs.

13 Saving the environment

Activity A

page 28

Vocabulary

green   concerned about protecting the environment
repaired   made to work again; mended
recycled   processed to be used again in a different form
nonrenewable   unable to be replaced by growing more
overpackaged   wrapped in too many layers of plastic and paper
low-energy   using less energy than other similar products
program   an organized plan of action

1 Work alone

If you want to free up some class time, ask students to take the quiz at home and bring their results to class.

2 Join a partner

Arrange students into an even number of pairs, and have them compare their answers.

3 Join another pair

Have pairs join together to continue the discussion.

Activity B

page 29

Vocabulary

chipped   having a small piece broken off
label   a piece of paper stuck onto something that gives information about it
storage   keeping something packed until it is needed
leftovers   cooked food that is kept for another meal
to wrap   to put something around food to protect it and keep it fresh
saucepan   a pan used to heat foods

1 Listen 🔲

1. Play the tape, pausing between each item to give students time to write. They only have to write down one answer for each item.

2. Play the tape again, if necessary. Some of the recycling ideas presented here may be unfamiliar to your students and should generate discussion in preparation for Activity B2.

see next page for answers

Answers

Item	One way to recycle
1. old reports	use them for note paper; good for taking phone messages
2. a chipped cup	put pens and pencils in it (and keep it on your desk); put flowers in it and use it as a vase
3. a used envelope	reuse it: cover the old address with a label and put a bigger stamp over the old one
4. an empty container	for storage: put leftover food in it for freezing; put cookies in it
5. used aluminum foil	reuse it: wrap food in it; wrap your lunch in it; cover a saucepan with it

Transcript   2 minutes 30 seconds

One.

MAN: Hey, are you going to throw all that away?

WOMAN: Yeah, uh . . . they've been used. They're old. We don't need them any more.

MAN: Yeah, but you can use them again. See, what I do sometimes is uh . . . I take them, and I cut them up into smaller pieces. (Huh.) Yeah, it makes great note paper, and . . . uh . . . they're also good for taking phone messages at home. . . . Oh, you can also reuse the other side of each page. Uh . . . It works out great.

WOMAN: Hey, that's a great idea. Thanks.

MAN: Sure.

Two.

WOMAN 1: Oh, don't throw that away!

WOMAN 2: Why not? It's chipped.

WOMAN 1: Well, I know it's chipped, but it's still good. There are lots of other things you could use it for. Like, um . . . you could put pens and pencils in it and (Huh.) keep it on your desk. Or you could put flowers in it and use it as a vase.

WOMAN 2: Hey, that's a good idea.

WOMAN 1: Yeah.

Three.

WOMAN 1: Don't throw that away!

WOMAN 2: Why not? It's been used already, and I'm finished with it. I sure can't use it again.

WOMAN 1: But if it's a strong one, you *can* reuse it.

WOMAN 2: What do you mean?

WOMAN 1: Well, you get a new label and you put it on top of the old address, and then you can buy a bigger stamp and put it on top of the old stamp.

WOMAN 2: Oh, wow. I never thought of that. That's a great idea.

Four.

WOMAN: Oh, hey, wait a second! Don't throw that away!

MAN: Why not? It's empty.

WOMAN: Well, yeah, but you can use it again. It's great for storage. You can put leftovers in there and freeze them. And you can put cookies in there – with the plastic lid on, they keep really fresh.

MAN: Hmm. Good idea. I'll hold on to it.

Five.

MAN: Hey, what are you doing? Don't throw that away.

WOMAN: Well, I've finished what I was eating.

MAN: Yeah, but you can . . . you can use that again. You know, you just unfold it, you know, make it flat, and you can wrap food with it, or you could, you know, wrap your lunch in it, or you could cover a saucepan with it. I mean, you know, there's lots of uses for that stuff.

2 Join a partner

Have students compare their answers and discuss the questions. They do not have to limit new recycling ideas to the items presented in Activity B1.

Sample answers

Other ideas for creative recycling include:

Some highlighters are refillable. You buy refills from an office-supply store. You push the ink cartridge onto the end of the highlighter and squeeze the ink into the old, empty highlighter – then it's as good as new.

Washing out glass jars and storing food in them, or filling them with stones or shells to use as decoration or to give away as presents.

Making book covers from old brown paper bags. The book covers help protect the books.

3 Group work

The photos show a wind farm, people planting a tree, and people binding newspapers for recycling. Have groups discuss the questions and then report back to the entire class about their conclusions.

Sample answers

What the photo shows	Benefits to the environment
(left photo) a wind farm	Wind can be used to create electricity – it's a renewable energy source that causes little or no pollution.
(middle photo) people planting a tree	Trees produce oxygen for us to breathe; the roots of a tree keep the soil from eroding (washing away); trees create shade from the sun and help people stay cool without having to use extra energy.
(right photo) people recycling newspapers	The newspapers can be used for making recycled paper instead of taking up space in landfills or being burned.

Communication task

Vocabulary

garbage   waste material that is being thrown away
smog   air pollution caused by the gases from cars reacting with sunlight

Procedure

Be sure to look at the two tasks (Task 8 on page C-6 and Task 17 on page C-10) before the lesson so that you can answer any questions that may arise. In this task, one student will describe environmental problems and the other will offer solutions.

Writing activity

Give students the following directions for a writing task:

Write about an idea you have for recycling something or avoiding waste. How creative can you be?

14 Going places

Unit 7, *Travel and transportation*, consists of Lessons 14–16. It focuses on vacations, different modes of transportation, and the characteristics of various countries.

Activity A

page 30

Vocabulary

chore   a job that has to be done around the house, such as cleaning and washing dishes
scared   frightened
to pick fruit   to take fruit from trees or bushes
neighbor   a person who lives near you
grandma   grandmother
company   people to be with so that you do not get lonesome
yucky (informal)   unpleasant
backpack   a large bag carried on one's back
backpacking   going hiking with a backpack
thunderstorm   a heavy rainstorm with lightning and thunder
Appalachian Trail   the name of a hiking trail in the eastern United States

1 Pair work

Have students discuss the pictures. This activity will encourage students to develop expectations about what they're going to hear in Activity A2.

2 Listen 📼

1. Play the tape. Pause the tape between each speaker.
2. Remind students that in this activity they are only listening for the number of the description for each picture.

Answers

4 (Tom), 2 (Robert), 3 (Marni), 1 (Wanda)

Transcript   4 minutes 40 seconds

The four descriptions are recorded twice on the tape.

One. Wanda.
WANDA: I spent the week with my grandparents in the country. They live . . . um . . . on a big farm, and they have chickens and lots of animals and fruit trees and fresh vegetables, and it's just really, really beautiful and peaceful. When I was there, . . . um . . . the apples were in season, and we went picking. And the neighbors came, and they helped pick the apples, and we packed them, and it was so much fun. And then at the end of the day, my grandma would cook a big meal, and we would just sit around and eat and eat and talk, and everything was delicious. It was so good. And I thought I'd be bored because they don't have a TV or anything, but I wasn't. It was . . . it was a lot of fun.

But at the end of the week, I just . . . I don't know, to tell you the truth, I really missed my friends, and . . . I think I

transcript continues on next page

prefer to live in the city, I – it's noisy and it's dirty in the city, but I . . . I like it better than the country. You know, the country's OK for a visit, but . . . um . . . it's too quiet for me!

Two. Robert.

ROBERT: My friend from Canada was in town last week, and I showed him around. And . . . uh . . . it was really fun. I thought it was going to be, you know, a bit of a drag, you know, taking him here and there, but . . . um . . . I ended up seeing a part of my town that I'd never seen before. Uh . . . We went to the zoo, . . . uh . . . we went to museums that I had never seen before. And . . . uh . . . we also went to the opera one night – oh, my gosh, it was just beautiful, and I had never been to the opera before.

You know, when someone from out of town comes to visit, you end up doing things in your own city that you've never thought of doing before. It was really great. The only thing is . . . uh . . . if I had it all to do all over again, I probably would plan out an itinerary for exactly what we'd do on what day because some days we spent, you know, a couple of hours just trying to figure out what to do.

Three. Marni.

MARNI: My family went away on vacation. I had some studying to do so I couldn't go with them. So I spent the week alone in the apartment. Every morning was so wonderfully peaceful – no alarm clock waking me up, no phone ringing, nothing. I had the whole day to myself. And in the mornings, I would do a lot of studying before lunch. And then after lunch, I would go jogging in the park or swimming or something like that. Every night I went to the movies, and I had a great time. I really wasn't lonely because I met my friends. Sometimes they'd go to the movies with me or meet me at the swimming pool. Anyway, I had company when I wanted it, and I didn't really miss my family – except I had to do all the

cooking and cleaning and yucky stuff like that.

Well, when my family got back, I acted really glad to see them, of course. But to tell you the truth, if they go away on vacation again, I think I'm going to stay home if I can.

Four. Tom.

TOM: OK, so my friends, they convinced me to go on this . . . uh . . . this hiking trip through the mountains. Uh . . . Eight of us, we were going to go for a week, you know, . . . hiking through the mountains, you know, backpacking, carrying all the gear on us, you know, so that, you know, we could camp out and, you know, cook, you know, over a fire and everything.

So we ended up camping out every single night, you know. And . . . uh . . . it was . . . uh – two of the nights were . . . were really nice because it was clear, . . . you know, the sky was clear so you could see all the stars. I mean, it was fantastic. I've never seen so many stars, you know. Uh . . . It was beautiful. And it was warm, and it was nice and everything and – Of course, you know, it couldn't be perfect. We did have a . . . on the la– I think it was the las– the second-to-last night, we had a . . . a huge thunderstorm. It scared us to death. You know, we were out there in the middle of nowhere, and we were soaking wet and scared, but it . . . it was OK because the next day it was warm, sunny, and all of our stuff got to dry out and everything, so it worked . . . it worked out OK.

And the whole trip was, you know, I'd have to say, was a good time. We . . . we covered about . . . uh . . . two hundred miles, I think, in one week. You know, we were really moving. Th-th-they're talking about doing it again next summer, so . . . uh . . . I'll probably do it. They're talking about the Appalachian Trail, but I . . . I mean that's over two thousand miles long, you know!

3 Listen again 📼

1. Have students preview the questions in the chart before listening to the tape again. Tell them that there is only one answer for each item.
2. Pause the tape between each speaker. You may want to have students compare their answers in pairs before they hear the next speaker.

Answers

See pages 53–54 for a transcript of this activity.

Who . . . ?	Wanda	Robert	Marni	Tom
didn't miss his/her family			✔	
didn't enjoy doing the chores			✔	
expected to be bored – but wasn't	✔			
went to the zoo		✔		
got wet and scared				✔
missed his/her friends	✔			
picked fruit	✔			
enjoyed watching the stars				✔
studied			✔	
thinks the country is too quiet	✔			
walked 200 miles in a week				✔
went jogging or swimming every day			✔	
went to the opera		✔		
wished he/she had planned ahead better		✔		

4 Join a partner

Have students discuss the questions in pairs.

Activity B	**Group work**
page 31	1. Arrange students into groups of three or four to complete the activity.
	2. Have students look at the photos and discuss the questions. It may be unlikely that they could really go to any of the places shown, but everyone likes to fantasize!

Activity C	**Communication task** 
page 31	**Vocabulary**

snapshot   a photograph
to have in common   to share similarities

Procedure

1. Be sure to look at the two tasks (Task 6 on page C-4 and Task 9 on page C-6) before the lesson so that you can answer any questions that may arise. This activity works a little differently from the previous communication tasks, so please read the directions carefully.

2. Split the class up into an even number of pairs. In this activity, both students in a pair will be looking at the same task at the same time. They will be working together to develop a story. Half the pairs should look at Task 6, and the other half at Task 9.

3. Check to make sure students are completing their stories. When they are ready, put the pairs into larger groups – each group of four should consist of pairs who were looking at different tasks. The pairs then take turns telling their stories. Don't spoil the game by telling students that one of the scenes is the same in each task.

Writing activity

Give students the following directions for a writing task:

Describe your most memorable or enjoyable vacation.

Activity A

page 32

Vocabulary

transportation   the system of buses, trains, airplanes, and other vehicles that people use to travel on

1 Pair work

1. Arrange students into an even number of pairs.

2. Have students discuss the statistics in the chart and compare their personal experiences of traveling by different forms of transportation.

Answers

People travel the most by . . .   car in South Korea.
                                  bus in Japan.
                                  train in Japan.
                                  air in the U.S.A.
People travel the least by . . . car in Brazil.
                                  bus in the U.S.A.
                                  train in the U.S.A.
                                  air in Brazil.

2 Join another pair

1. Combine pairs into groups.

2. Encourage students to do more than just say "by bus" in describing how they get to class. Describe your journey to class, door-to-door (for example: "I leave my house, turn right, and walk down the street to the main road. There's a bus stop just at the end of my street. I wait for the Number 31 bus to come and I get on. When the bus gets to Main Street, I get off. I have to walk three blocks east until I get to Fourth Avenue and then . . .").

   The more thorough students are in describing their commutes, the more easily they can compare the relative difficulty of one another's trips.

3 Group work

1. Have students stay in the same groups to work out the story behind each picture.

2. Reassemble the class and ask students from various groups to tell everyone what they think the story is behind a particular picture.

Vocabulary

You may want to see if students can describe the vehicles listed in the yellow box on page 33 before you pre-teach the vocabulary.

> **station wagon**   a car with a lot of space behind the back seats and a large door in the back
>
> **pickup truck**   a car with one row of seats and an open part at the back for carrying things
>
> **convertible**   a car with a roof that folds back
>
> **hatchback**   a car with a door at the back that opens upwards
>
> **souvenir**   something you buy to remind you of a place you have visited

Group work

1. Have students discuss the questions. Those who are too young to drive have been passengers in cars and also might hope to learn to drive eventually, so they will have views and ideas to express.

2. After students have discussed all the questions, ask each group to tell the rest of the class the most interesting points that came up in their discussion. The idea that people often buy a particular kind of car to make a statement about themselves is one that some students may want to pursue.

3. Write up a list of cars that are popular in each student's country, and ask them to say what kind of person would own each one.

Before the next lesson

Make sure that everyone notices the instructions on the bottom of page 33. Students will need to bring an item to class in order for Activity D on page 36 to work. Students who cannot bring items from "home" because they are studying far from home can participate by bringing photographs they've taken or gifts that they have bought and plan to take back with them.

16 What's it like there?

Activity A

page 34

1 Pair work

1. Form an even number of pairs.

2. Have students look at the pictures and describe them using the words in the vocabulary box. Go around helping with additional vocabulary.

3. Ask the class which country or countries they think the photos show. After students volunteer their ideas, you can reveal that all three photos are of different places in the same country: Australia. Did anyone guess this?

2 Join another pair

1. Combine pairs into groups. Draw students' attention to the useful phrases in the speech balloon.

2. After the discussion, ask various students to tell the rest of the class which country they would most like to visit and why.

Activity B

page 35

Vocabulary

region   a part of a country
authentic   showing the true nature of a person, place, or thing
humid   with a lot of tiny drops of water in the air
monsoon season   a period of heavy rain during the summer in certain parts of Asia
temple   a building used for worship in some religions, such as Buddhism
sight-seeing   going to interesting places that tourists usually visit
to impress someone   to make someone admire you
bracelet   a piece of jewelry that you wear around your wrist

1 Listen 📼

1. Tell your students you are writing some names on the board so that they will know how to pronounce them. Write the names in alphabetical order and don't tell your students what person or place they refer to in the recording: Acropolis, Bangkok, Chiang Mai, Frida Kahlo, Parthenon, Phuket, the Plaka, Diego Rivera, Taxco

2. Play the tape, pausing between each speaker to give students time to write. You may also want to have them compare their answers in pairs between speakers. You'll probably need to play the tape more than once for students to get all the answers.

3. It shouldn't be too difficult for students to guess which countries were being talked about. Encourage them to explain how they guessed. Ask them if the speakers gave them clues or if they knew something about the countries already.

see next page for answers

Activity B **Answers**

page 35
continued

Jackie
1. hot and humid; rained a little bit every day
2. the food (spicy and delicious)
3. Bangkok: incredible shopping; the city is so alive; culturally interesting; beautiful temples
4. Thailand

Nick
1. a lot of sight-seeing
2. staying with his relatives; going to places tourists wouldn't know about
3. to impress his relatives with what he has learned
4. Greece

Kate
1. perfect; wonderful; about 75 degrees every day; mostly sunny
2. seeing the work of Diego Rivera and Frida Kahlo
3. a silver bracelet
4. Mexico

Transcript   4 minutes 25 seconds

First, Jackie.

INTERVIEWER: Hey, so tell me about your trip. When were you there?

JACKIE: Ah . . . I was there last year, but I remember it like it was yesterday.

INTERVIEWER: Must have been great.

JACKIE: Oh, it was!

INTERVIEWER: So what's the weather like?

JACKIE: Well, . . . um . . . it was the beginning of June, so it was pretty hot and humid. And it was also the very beginning of monsoon season, so it rained for a little bit of every day. (Hmm.) But it was so beautiful, it didn't matter. (Uh-huh.) There was so much to see.

INTERVIEWER: Yeah, well, what about the food? Did you like the food?

JACKIE: Oh! The food was the best part of the trip. The food was so good. (Hmm.) It's . . . it's very, very spicy, but so delicious. Oh, and the interesting thing (Hmm.) is that they give you the spices separately, so you can choose how much of every spice you want to put on your food, (Oh.) so you can make it as hot as you want – or not so hot, if you don't want.

INTERVIEWER: Hmm. Neat. Which part of the country would you say you liked the most?

JACKIE: Wow. That's really difficult. I was . . . I was all over the place. Um . . . Well, in the north in Chiang Mai, it's so rural and beautiful. And . . . uh – oh, Phuket – Phuket is an island with beautiful beaches. It's so relaxing. But I think Bangkok was my favorite. Um . . . The shopping there is incredible. (Hmm.) The city is so alive. Oh, and culturally it is so interesting. The temples are so beautiful. It's . . . it's really – yeah, I'd say Bangkok – that was my favorite place.

Now, Nick.

INTERVIEWER: Hey, when did you go on your trip?

NICK: I went at the beginning of last summer, actually.

INTERVIEWER: Oh, tell me about it.

NICK: Well, I started out . . . uh . . . doing a lot of sight-seeing. (Mm-hmm.) I saw the Acropolis and the Parthenon. I saw the Olympic Stadium – it was really great. (Mm-hmm.) Um . . . I spent a lot of time in an area of the city called the

Plaka. It's got a lot of tavernas, which are really restaurants, and great shops and nightclubs. It's a fun place.

INTERVIEWER: Mm-hmm. Did you go to any other parts of the country during your trip?

NICK: Yeah, actually I . . . I went to the site of the first Olympics. Uh . . . I'm a big sports fan, so that was very interesting to me.

INTERVIEWER: Mm-hmm.

NICK: And I spent some time on the islands. Uh . . . They were beautiful, just beautiful.

INTERVIEWER: Hmm. What was your favorite part of the trip?

NICK: Well, you know, I . . . I have relatives there, (Mm-hmm.) and . . . uh . . . I stayed with them, and that was really nice because I got a chance to, you know, look around without really being a tourist. You know, they . . . they took me places that, you know, tourists wouldn't even necessarily know about. So that was . . . that was nice.

INTERVIEWER: Well, would you go back?

NICK: Oh, absolutely! I'd love to see my relatives again. You know, before . . . before I went, I . . . I couldn't speak the language, so I had, you know, some difficulty communicating with them, and now that I got back, I've . . . I've actually been taking some lessons, and I'd just love to go back and impress them with what I've learned.

Finally, Kate.

INTERVIEWER: When did you go on your trip?

KATE: Oh, well, let's see. . . . Um . . . It's two years ago now.

INTERVIEWER: Oh. How was the weather?

KATE: Well, I was there in the spring, you know, March-April, (Mm-hmm.) and it was perfect! It was so wonderful, about seventy-five degrees every day, mostly sunny, and it only rained once, just a little bit.

INTERVIEWER: Mmm. Well, what did you like the most about your trip?

KATE: Well, you know, I'm an artist, (Mm-hmm.) so of course I wanted to see the work of the great painter Diego Rivera. You know, he painted a lot of murals, and I tried to see as many as I could when I was there. Oh, and I also love Frida Kahlo. I love *her* work, and so I went to the Frida Kahlo Museum. (Hmm.) That was terrific.

INTERVIEWER: Uh-huh. What did you do besides go to museums?

KATE: Well, I went to a lovely little city called Taxco. (Hmm.) Do you know Taxco?

INTERVIEWER: No.

KATE: It's this small city in the mountains with beautiful old buildings and architecture. And it is also *the* place to go for silverwork. (Ah.) All over Taxco there are little stores that sell handmade silver jewelry. And I bought this bracelet there. I just love it.

2 Group work

1. Have students make a short list of the sights and cities that tourists visit in their countries before they begin their discussion. The most interesting question is probably the last one. Make sure students have time to discuss it.

2. After the discussion, reassemble the class and ask various students to give a brief report to the rest of the class.

Vocabulary

Many of the missing words in the listening activity are defined in the vocabulary list. You may want to wait and answer vocabulary questions *after* students have completed the listening activity.

> **to paint an extraordinary picture** to describe in a very surprising way
> **unspoiled** not visited by tourists; unchanged
> **wilderness** a natural, uninhabited area
> **fjord** a long strip of sea between steep hills
> **majestic** large, beautiful, and impressive
> **village** a group of houses in the countryside, smaller than a town
> **lush green meadow** a green field
> **towering** very high
> **fairest climate** the most wonderful weather conditions
> **diversity** variety (of climates and things to do)
> **coupon** a small part of a magazine or newspaper that you can cut out, write your name and address on, and send off in order to get something back

1 Read/listen 📼

1. Ask your students to read the article and guess the missing words before coming to class. If it is not possible to assign the reading for homework, allow plenty of class time for students to complete the task working in pairs.

2. Play the tape so students can check their work.

3. Ask students if they would like to suggest other possible word choices (for example, *fields* or *pastures* for *meadows*). Evaluate their suggestions.

Transcript and answers   1 minute 5 seconds

Missing words are in bold type.

This is what New Zealand looks like to the experienced traveler. A **world** traveler who tries to describe New Zealand is apt to paint an extraordinary **picture**. He'll begin by telling you it has the unspoiled **wilderness** of Alaska, beaches that rival Hawaii, breathtakingly **beautiful** fjords like Norway, and majestic Alps like Switzerland. Then, to confuse things a little more, he'll tell you New Zealand's cities and **villages** will make you think of England, New Zealand's lush green **meadows** will remind you of Ireland, and her towering Mt. Egmont will bring to mind Japan's Mt. Fuji. To top it off, he'll say New Zealand has the **nicest** people, fairest climate, and **cleanest** air on all the green earth. And on all counts, he'll be right. For the full story about New Zealand's diversity, **send** in this coupon.

2 Pair work

Have students discuss the questions. There are six places besides New Zealand mentioned in the advertisement, and you can ask your students to think of what other things the six places are famous for.

Sample answers

Place	Famous for ...	Also famous for ...
Alaska	wilderness	the Inuit/Eskimo people, oil, wildlife, glaciers, snow
Hawaii	beaches	sunshine, surfing, volcanoes, good weather, islands, luaus (Hawaiian feasts)
Norway	fjords	snow, midnight sun, fishing, cross-country skiing
Switzerland	Alps	watches, cuckoo clocks, chocolate
England	cities and villages	roast beef and Yorkshire pudding, the Royal family, castles
Ireland	meadows	friendly people, rain, writers and poets
Japan	Mount Fuji	temples, cities, fast trains, sushi

3 Pair work

1. Brainstorm the names of some countries if necessary, and write them on the board. Students can then pick the three they know most about.

2. After students have completed the chart, combine pairs so that groups of students can compare what they've written.

3. Finish by asking students to explain which foreign country they'd most like to visit and why.

Activity D

page 36

Group work

See notes on this activity under the "Before the next lesson" section of Lesson 15, Activity B.

Activity E

page 36

Communication task

Vocabulary

sq km   square kilometer
sq mi   square mile
population density   the number of people in a given area
°F   degrees Fahrenheit
°C   degrees Celsius
land mass   land area

procedure continues on next page

Procedure

1. Be sure to look at the two tasks (Task 7 on page C-5 and Task 18 on page C-11) before the lesson so that you can answer any questions that may arise.

2. Have students form groups of four. Two students in each group will look at the first task while the other two will look at the second. Go around the class and help each pair with any questions they may have about the statistics.

3. Ask the four students to work together to answer the questions.

Answers

1. Canada
2. New Zealand
3. Republic of Ireland
4. Australia
5. Canada
6. Australia, Canada

Writing activities

Give students the following directions for a writing task:

Write one or more paragraphs about the photographs, postcards, souvenir, or gift you brought to class. Explain the story behind your item.

Write a description of your own country in the same style as the descriptions in Task 7 (on page C-5) and Task 18 (on page C-11).

Review puzzles

page 37

The vocabulary in Puzzle A is from Lessons 8–13. The vocabulary in Puzzle B is from Lessons 14–16.

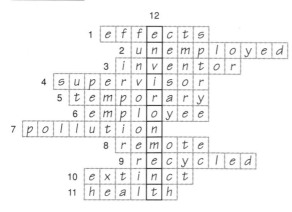

Puzzle A

```
                    12
 1  e f f e c t s
 2  u n e m p l o y e d
 3  i n v e n t o r
 4  s u p e r v i s o r
 5  t e m p o r a r y
 6  e m p l o y e e
 7  p o l l u t i o n
 8  r e m o t e
 9  r e c y c l e d
10  e x t i n c t
11  h e a l t h
```

Puzzle B

```
                        17
 1  v a c a t i o n
 2  t r a n s p o r t a t i o n
 3  s e d a n
 4  l i m o u s i n e
 5  t r a v e l e r
 6  s i g h t - s e e i n g
 7  t o u r i s t
 8  b e a c h
 9  s o u v e n i r
10  s k y s c r a p e r
11  p o s t c a r d s
12  c o u n t r y
13  t r i p
14  d e s e r t
15  c h o r e s
16  a t t r a c t i o n s
```

17 What do you enjoy doing?

Unit 8, *Leisure time*, consists of Lessons 17–18. It focuses on leisure activities and interests.

Note that the terms *hobbies* and *interests* are used interchangeably in this lesson to designate activities that students enjoy doing in their free, or leisure, time. Students may need fairly technical vocabulary to talk about the hobbies they have, so you may need to allow extra time to work on vocabulary.

Activity A

page 38

Vocabulary

hobbies   something you do in your spare time
yoga   mental and physical activities that give you control over your mind and body
science fiction   referring to books or movies about the future and space travel
home game   a baseball game that is played on your own team's playing field
gym   a hall where you do exercises
bird-watching   the hobby of observing birds in nature
classifying   dividing into groups according to type
to compile   to collect information from different sources
bead making   making jewelry with small, round pieces of glass or wood that have holes through them
semiprecious gem   a jewel that is not as valuable as a precious gem such as a diamond, emerald, or ruby
meditation   thinking calmly and quietly as a way of relaxing your mind
by one's own steam   by one's own energy and effort
tranquil   calm; peaceful

1 Pair work

Ask students to identify the activities and then say which ones they enjoy or which ones they *think* they would/wouldn't enjoy. The silhouettes are deliberately ambiguous to generate discussion. This activity serves as a warm-up for the listening activity that follows.

Answers

top row: reading, yoga, stamp-collecting, weight-lifting, playing with children
bottom row: bird-watching, cycling/bicycling, baseball, walking/hiking, jewelry making

procedure continues on next page

2 Listen 🔲

Pause the tape between each interview. During the first listening, students only have to fill in the *first* column. Please note that while other activities may be mentioned on the tape, students should concentrate on the speakers' "favorites" only.

Answers for A2 and A3

	Favorite hobbies or interests?	What do you enjoy most about each activity?	How long do you spend on each activity?
Wanda	1. walking	being out in nature	two hours a day
	2. yoga	very centering, relaxing, and fun	one hour in the morning, a half hour at night
Robert	1. baseball	family and friends can get together and have a good time	two hours practice every afternoon plus games every Sunday
	2. science fiction	reading about UFOs	one hour every night
Christopher	1. going to the gym	feels healthy; enjoys being with friends	one and a half to two hours, four times a week
	2. bird-watching	most relaxing thing he does; enjoys classifying birds	three or four hours, twice a week
Sheila	1. bike riding	great exercise; loves the sense of freedom and the feeling she gets afterward; loves going somewhere by her own steam	two to three hours a day and more on the weekends
	2. jewelry making	wonderful meditation, tranquil and calming; very concrete, "hands on"; have beautiful jewelry	between five and eight hours a week

Transcript   5 minutes 30 seconds

The four conversations are recorded twice on the tape.

Wanda.

INTERVIEWER: Uh, Wanda, what sort of interests do you have? What do you do in your free time?

WANDA: Well, I love to take long walks in nature, and I'm really into yoga – I do a lot of yoga.

INTERVIEWER: What do you enjoy most about those activities?

WANDA: Well, walking – I love being out in nature . . . um . . . looking at the trees and the birds and all different kinds of people, and just feeling my body move, and . . . you know, the wind hitting my face. I just like being outdoors. And yoga – it's very centering for me and very relaxing, too. I go through about ten different positions, and it's really . . . it's really fun.

INTERVIEWER: And how long do you spend on those sort of activities?

WANDA: Well, yoga I do for about an hour in the morning and a half hour at night. And walking – I try to get in at least two hours of strenuous walking a day.

INTERVIEWER: Boy, that's great. You must keep really fit.

WANDA: I try, I try.

Robert.

INTERVIEWER: Hi, Robert, what do you do in your free time? What sort of hobbies do you have?

ROBERT: Well, . . . um . . . I'm very interested in athletics. I play all kinds of sports after school . . . uh . . . my favorite being baseball. And . . . um . . . I'm also a big reader of science fiction.

INTERVIEWER: And what do you enjoy most about those things?

ROBERT: Well, . . . uh . . . baseball has been . . . uh . . . a part of my life since childhood. It's a time for family and friends to get together and have a good time. We spend . . . um . . . you know, every spring and summer afternoon playing baseball. Uh . . . We'd go down to the Little League and play, and when I went to school, then there'd be the home games . . . um . . . under the lights at night, and my whole family would be there. And it'd be just, you know, a great time with great memories. And . . . um . . . as far as science fiction goes, . . . uh . . . my favorite thing about that is just reading about UFOs. Um . . . My . . . uh . . . literature teacher turned me on to science fiction, and . . . um . . . I read a few . . . uh . . . science-fiction novels in her class, and ever since I've been hooked on science fiction.

INTERVIEWER: And how long do you get to spend on those things?

ROBERT: Well, every afternoon we have practice for about two hours . . . uh . . . that's baseball practice, and then we have games every Sunday. Um . . . And . . . um . . . I read for about an hour before bed every night.

Christopher.

INTERVIEWER: Hi, Christopher, what do you do in your free time? What sort of hobbies do you have?

CHRISTOPHER: Well, I have a lot of hobbies. I like to read, and I like to work on computers. Probably my two favorites, though, are going to the gym and bird-watching. They're both two hobbies that balance each other well because one is inside and one is outside, so it doesn't matter what the weather's like, I can always do one.

INTERVIEWER: And what do you enjoy most about each activity?

CHRISTOPHER: Well, when I go to the gym, . . . I usually go in the morning. So when I do, it makes the rest of the day feel much better. I feel healthy, and I feel good, and I also have a lot of friends at the gym, and so I enjoy being with them. Bird-watching – well, it's a ni– it's the

transcript continues on next page

most relaxing thing I do during my week. I enjoy classifying birds, and I keep lists and compile lists of where I've seen the birds and . . . and . . . and what birds I've seen.

INTERVIEWER: How long do you spend on each activity?

CHRISTOPHER: When I go to the gym, I try to go for an hour and a half or two hours. I try to go about four times a week. And bird-watching, I go . . . I try to always go twice a week when I can, and I try to spend at least three or four hours when I do that.

Sheila.

INTERVIEWER: Sheila, what do you do with your free time? Uh . . . What are your interests?

SHEILA: I love sports. Whenever I can, I like to . . . uh . . . to go out with my bike, take a nice bike ride. When I can't get outdoors and when I'm . . . uh . . . in . . . in the house, . . . uh . . . I . . . I love to make jewelry. I have a hobby of . . . uh . . . bead making with . . . uh . . . semiprecious gems that I . . . I spend a lot of time at that as well.

INTERVIEWER: And what would you say that . . . uh . . . that you enjoy most about each of those activities?

SHEILA: Oh, boy, . . . um . . . riding a bike is . . . uh . . . great exercise. I love the sense of freedom . . . and . . . and the . . . uh – it's almost like moving meditation. Um . . . I love th-the feeling I get after a hard bike ride, and . . . uh . . . and I love being able to get somewhere by my own steam. It's a wonderful feeling. (Mm-hmm.) Um . . . The jewelry making is . . . a wonderful . . . uh . . . a wonderful meditation in that it's very tranquil, it's very calming, and at the end of your time, you have a beautiful necklace or a beautiful pair of earrings to show for it. It's very . . . it's very concrete. It's very "hands on." That's what I love about jewelry making.

INTERVIEWER: How long would you say you spend on each of those activities?

SHEILA: I would say . . . um . . . I'm on the bike every day probably between two and three hours . . . uh . . . more on the weekends. (Mm-hmm.) And for the jewelry making . . . I probably spend between five and eight hours a week, whenever I have the time.

3 Listen again

1. Point out to students that when the speakers mention several reasons why they enjoy an activity, they only need to note down one of them.

2. Pause the tape between each interview. Students will probably need to hear the tape at least two times to get all the answers.

3. Have students compare answers in pairs and/or review the answers as a class. In either case, tell students that there may be some variations in answers, depending on one's interpretation of the speakers' reasons.

Vocabulary

rock climbing   going up a cliff or mountain by a challenging vertical route
ballooning   being carried in the air in a basket that is hanging from a hot-air balloon

1 Pair work

Have students discuss the questions. Encourage students who have tried these activities to tell the class what they enjoy about them.

2 Work alone

1. Invite students to engage in a few moments of silent contemplation and to make notes. If they don't do this, the questions for the ensuing pair-work activity are likely to fall flat.

2. Go around the class giving individual help with vocabulary as necessary.

3 Join a partner

Find out how many different hobbies or interests are represented in the class. Students will enjoy talking about whose hobby they think is the most unusual and which hobby is the most popular. Ask them to speculate on why a particular hobby is so popular.

Activity C

page 39

Communication task

Vocabulary

skydiving   jumping out of an airplane with a parachute

Procedure

1. Be sure to look at the two tasks (Task 19 on page C-12 and Task 29 on page C-17) before the lesson so that you can answer any questions that may arise.

2. Have students work in pairs, with one member of the pair looking at Task 19 and the other member at Task 29. There's no need to explain the vocabulary – the hobbies are illustrated in the tasks, and it's up to the students to explain them if their partners don't know what they are. The students should write down each other's answers.

3. After the pair work is finished, find out from the class how many people have actually tried each activity. As a class, discuss the various reasons students want/don't want to try the activities.

Writing activity

Give students the following directions for a writing task:

Write a letter to a friend. In your letter, describe your favorite leisure activity and why you enjoy it. Ask your friend to try it with you the next time you meet and give reasons why he or she should try it.

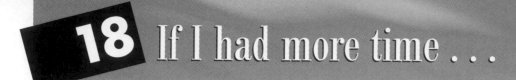

18 If I had more time . . .

Activity A

page 40

Vocabulary

cleaning house   doing household chores, such as dusting, tidying, vacuuming, and polishing

statistics   information based on the number of times something happens; a collection of numbers that gives information about something

unbelievable   difficult to believe; very surprising

the average person   a typical person, according to statistics

1 Pair work

Allow some extra time to explain this activity to students, as the idea of compressing a lifetime into a week may be confusing. The hours listed here add up to 304.5 hours, which is obviously more hours than there are in a week. But many of the hours overlap (for example, most of a person's hours in bed are spent at home and many hours at work are often spent in meetings). The 6 hours per week in school is averaged out over a lifetime (most people spend a limited number of years in school and then go to work – remember, this figure is averaged out over a lifetime). Leave it to the students to analyze the information. Students should not only consider the number of hours listed here, but also the types of activities listed and the order in which they are presented. Note that, expressed in years, the figures are even more impressive. In a lifetime the average person spends about 52 years at home, 26 years in bed, 10 years at work, 7 years in the bathroom, and 6 years watching TV!

2 Work alone

Encourage students to add activities to the list. If they choose to, they can estimate how many hours they think the average person spends doing each activity; however, it isn't necessary that they include this information.

Sample answers

studying, cooking, reading, playing sports, watching sports, taking care of children, waiting at the doctor's or dentist's office, talking on the telephone, spending time with friends, doing errands, walking

3 Pair work

1. Have each student fill in information as it pertains to his or her life, discussing it with a partner as he or she works. Advise students that there's no need for extreme accuracy in filling in the chart.

2. Reassemble the class and have various students list some of the important activities they think are missing from the chart. Conclude the activity by discussing how students' hours compare with the hours of "the average person" listed in the chart.

Vocabulary

approximately   about

1 Pair work

Have students form an even number of pairs to do the activity. In Activity A the students talked about the number of hours in a week they spend doing various things. Now they will talk about how many times a month they do things.

2 Join another pair

1. Combine pairs and give them time to compare their findings.
2. Reassemble the class. Conclude the activity by working with students to identify which activities class members did the least number of times in the past month.

Writing activity

Give students the following directions for a writing task:

Describe a typical day in your life. What do you do? Where do you go? How much time do you spend on different activities during the day?

19 Playing and watching sports

Unit 9, *Games and sports*, consists of Lessons 19–20.

This lesson focuses on different kinds of sports as well as the advantages of exercise as a way of keeping fit. Many of the topics presented are also of interest to those students who don't play sports.

Activity A
page 42

Vocabulary

to participate   to take part in; to play

1 Pair work

1. Answer any questions students may have about the words in the vocabulary box.
2. Arrange students into an even number of pairs to talk about the photos.

2 Join another pair

Combine pairs into groups. Give students time to discuss the questions. Students who don't like sports have a chance to say why not in this activity.

Activity B
page 43

Vocabulary

healthy practice   something you do that is good for you
vegetarian   a person who does not eat meat or fish
vegetarian diet   the foods regularly eaten by a vegetarian

1 Listen 🔲

1. Before playing the tape, ask students to brainstorm together to name some advantages of each healthy practice listed in the chart. This should help prepare them for the lengthy listening passage that will follow.
2. Play the tape, pausing it after each speaker to give everyone enough time to write. If you decide to allow students to discuss their answers with a partner before putting them in writing, play the tape only once and tell students beforehand that that is what you plan to do.
3. Play the tape a second time if students are struggling. Another option: Have the students vote on the two speakers they'd like to hear again and replay that section of the tape only. Students do not need to understand every word to complete this activity.

Answers

Students need to note down only one advantage for each item.

1. yoga	calming; can shut out the world for awhile; you use all your muscles
2. swimming	works out your whole body; engages your breathing fully; safe because it's nonimpact – you don't hurt your bones or muscles

3. running   great for your heart and your whole body; great way to meet people; good to be out in the sunshine

4. walking   keeps you fit; gets rid of stress; no accidents or pulled necks or muscles; can look around at the shops, see the people, take in the atmosphere

5. basketball   great workout; a lot of fun

6. vegetarian diet   live a longer life; feel more energized

Transcript   4 minutes

One.

INTERVIEWER: What do you do to keep fit?

LORI: Well, lately I've taken up yoga, and it seems to be a great thing for me because I tend to move really fast in my daily life, and . . . uh . . . yoga seems to be really calming for me. It's very slow, it's very tranquil, and I just am forced to breathe and to move slowly. In fact, one of the . . . one of the . . . uh . . . elements of yoga is "It doesn't matter, nothing matters, you're here with yourself now, it's all in the breath." So I really . . . uh . . . I think that's a good balance for me. I really can . . . can . . . shut the world out for a while. I mean, the workout is . . . is . . . harder than you would think. It's actually . . . um . . . quite challenging. And you – they say in yoga that you use every . . . every . . . group of muscles in your body.

Two.

INTERVIEWER: What do you do to keep fit?

TERRY: Well, you know they say that swimming is the best, most total exercise because it works out your whole body. So, you know, you're not isolating any particular muscle group, your whole body's getting a workout. And it really engages your breathing very fully. So when you're done, you feel tired, but in a very satisfying way. It's one of the safest ways that you can exercise because it's nonimpact. You don't hurt your bones or your muscles. Swimming is great because I . . . you know, I'm my own boss. I just go whenever I can squeeze it in, even for ten minutes.

Three.

INTERVIEWER: What do you do to keep fit?

ROBERT: I'm a runner. You know, great for your heart, it's great for your whole body, you get out in the sun. Every morning I run at least . . . uh . . . five miles, and it's . . . uh . . . it's a great way to meet people, too. I go to the park and, you know, you have a good time out there in the sunshine before you go to work.

Four.

INTERVIEWER: What do you do to keep fit?

TREVOR: Well, I do a lot of walking. I walk everywhere. I walk – any appointment I have, I walk there, I don't take taxis at all or buses, I just leave early enough to get there, and . . . it's . . . it works out well. Obviously, I keep fit. I don't have any real stress. You know, sometimes people that go to the gym end up with accidents and pulled necks and pulled muscles, but that never happens to me. I take it very easy, and I think I get just as much of a workout, really. I don't know if there are any disadvantages. I . . . I look around the shops. I have a great time. I sort of see the people in the street and take in the atmosphere.

transcript continues on next page

Activity B

page 43 continued

Five.

INTERVIEWER: What do you do to keep fit?

CHRISTOPHER: Well, I like to run and . . . and . . . work out with weights, but mostly I like to play basketball. It's a great workout, first of all, but more than that, it's a lot of fun. I never get tired of it, so it's like doing something that you want to do. It's like eating broccoli and liking it at the same time. It's good for you, but it's fun, anyway. It's most fun when you get to play with a lot of other people, so it s-sometimes can be difficult getting a group of people who can all play at the same time and finding a court to play on. You can play by yourself, but it's not as enjoyable.

Six.

INTERVIEWER: What do you do to keep fit?

BILL: Oh, . . . um . . . mainly . . . I watch what I eat. I eat mostly a vegetarian diet. If you cut down on your meat and your fat intake, and . . . uh . . . you know, you make sure you get all your proper amino acids and proteins, then you're going to live a longer life, and you actually feel more energized when you eat that kind of food.

2 Join a partner

In small groups, have students compare their answers and give their personal reactions to what they've heard. Students will also have the chance to talk about any healthy practices that they engage in.

Activity C

page 43

Vocabulary

sports nut   a person who loves playing, watching, and talking about sports

1 Pair work

Spend some time going over unfamiliar vocabulary. Encourage students to add any favorite sports (for example, *table tennis* or *rugby* or *water-skiing*) and any national sports (for example, the Korean sport of *tae kwon do* or the Japanese sports of *kendo* and *aikido*) that are missing from the quiz.

Answers

do aerobics	play football	do judo	go surfing
play badminton	play golf	do karate	go swimming
play baseball	do gymnastics	go rock climbing	play tennis
play basketball	play hockey	go roller-skating	play volleyball
go bowling	go horseback riding	go sailing	go walking
go cycling	go ice-skating	go skiing	do weight lifting
go fishing	go jogging	play soccer	go windsurfing

2 Work alone

1. Explain the distinction between spectator sports and participatory sports for this activity.

2. Demonstrate the activity by writing the first two items on the board and saying how many times a year you participate in them.

74 | Games and sports

3 Join a partner

1. Ask students to add up their scores and turn to Task 34 on page C-20 to interpret those scores.

2. As students discuss the quiz in pairs, encourage them to disagree with the interpretations, which are (of course) very superficial.

3. Reassemble the class and find out how many members of the class are "sports nuts."

Follow-up activity

Sports activities have their own jargon. Have students look up some of the special terms that are used in their favorite sports, so that they can talk about these sports in greater detail. Here are various terms, some of which students who are sports fans might be interested in learning:

where you play	baseball field, tennis court, golf course, basketball court, boxing ring
time-keeping	time-out, first half, first quarter, interval, halftime
scoring	foul, penalty, free throw, score, points, shot, goal, tie
sports equipment	baseball bat, tennis racket, golf clubs, pool cue, boxing gloves
participants	team, side, player, opponent, spectators, crowd, coach, manager, trainer, contestant, pitcher, fielder, quarterback, substitute
officials	judge, referee, umpire
describing a game	exciting, thrilling, wonderful, disappointing, boring

Writing activity

Give students the following directions for a writing task:

Choose one of these writing activities:
Describe a sport you like to play (or watch) and explain why you enjoy it.
Write a description of a great game or match that you watched recently.

20 How about a game?

In this lesson, the word *game* excludes athletic sports, but includes games of chance and skill, and parlor games.

Activity A
page 44

Vocabulary

tile game   a game played with small pieces of wood or plastic, such as Scrabble or dominoes

party game   an amusing or silly game played at parties, such as charades

1 Pair work

Have the students look at the picture. Don't be surprised if students fail to recognize some of the games – just encourage them to talk about the ones they do know. All the games pictured can be found in the list for Activity A2.

Answers

The picture shows the following games, from the top left corner clockwise: chess, dominoes, a crossword puzzle, Monopoly, cards (below the chess board), Japanese flower cards (*hanafuda*), and a word-search puzzle.

2 Pair work

Have students add games to the list and answer the questions. Students should focus on games they are familiar with. You may want to look up some of the games yourself to become familiar with the basics.

Activity B
page 45

Vocabulary

adorable   lovable

1 Group work

1. Form groups of four to six students. Each group should choose one game to play.
2. Go around the class, making sure everyone knows what to do and how to play the various games.

2 Group work

1. Have each group choose a new game to play.
2. Reassemble the whole class so that students can compare experiences. If there's time the groups may want to play a third game, especially if a different group reports having had a lot of fun with it.

Activity C   Communication task

page 45

Procedure

1. Be sure to look at the three tasks (Task 24 on page C-15, Task 28 on page C-16, and Task 33 on page C-19) before the lesson so that you can answer any questions that may arise.

2. Remind students that only *yes/no* questions are allowed. All students have the same instructions for this task and will practice question formation while playing a game.

3. Make sure students also understand that the famous person can be someone who is alive or dead. If necessary, demonstrate by thinking of someone everyone in the class might know, and have them ask you questions to find out who you are.

Writing activity

Give students the following directions for a writing task:

Describe a game you like to play, and explain how it's played.

21 In the news

Unit 10, *News and current events*, consists of Lessons 21–22. It focuses on upbeat news stories that have happy endings.

Activity A

page 46

1 Pair work

Have students form an even number of pairs, and go around the class helping the students with any vocabulary they need. This is a vocabulary activity, as well as a warm-up for Activity B.

2 Join another pair

1. Combine pairs into groups of four.
2. Point out the expressions in the speech balloon.
3. After students have finished comparing ideas, ask for a short oral report from each group.

Activity B

page 47

Vocabulary

appendix a small part of the intestines that has no use
recovery getting better after an illness
shallow not deep
jet ski a small vehicle that rides on skis on water and is propelled by water power
high tide when the ocean has risen to its highest point
diver a person who goes under the water using special breathing equipment (also known as a scuba diver)
guiding showing the correct route
adopted taken into a family and raised as a member of that family
separate different; individual

1 Listen 🔲

Do not pause the tape between each report. Students will match each news report to a picture in Activity A1.

Answers

Number of the pictures, clockwise from the top: 1, 3, 4, 2

Transcript   3 minutes 15 seconds

The newscast is recorded twice on the tape.

KAREN: Hello and welcome to Channel Five News. I'm Karen Armstrong.

JIM: And I'm Jim Lopez. And today's main story is about the forest fires that started burning on Friday. Strong winds drove the flames towards the city, and by Saturday hundreds of families in Bellevue had to leave the area because the fire was very close to their homes. According to Fire Chief Andy Wallace, the fire is now under control. The wind has dropped so the fire will probably not get any closer to the city. Karen.

KAREN: A woman was rescued from a boat by helicopter late this afternoon. Mary Avona was out on her boat with some friends, when she started to have stomach pains. An hour later, the pains were worse, and she decided that she needed immediate medical attention. Ms. Avona and her friends were fifty miles off the coast and realized that it would take too long to sail back. Ms. Avona's friend radioed the Coast Guard, and a helicopter was sent to pick her up. She was taken to Memorial Hospital, and her appendix was removed in an emergency operation. Doctors say the operation was a success, and Ms. Avona will make a full recovery.

JIM: And another sea rescue is being attempted right now in Independence Bay. Here's Robin Alexander, live with the details.

ROBIN: I'm here at Independence Bay. At high tide on Friday night, a whale swam into the bay. But at low tide, the water was so shallow that it couldn't swim out again. Over the weekend, hundreds of sight-seers in boats and on jet skis went to see the whale. But the noise scared the animal so much that it got confused and couldn't find its way out to the open ocean at the next high tide. Now, a team of divers came to help the whale this morning. They eventually were able to calm the whale down. About an hour ago, they started guiding the whale towards the open ocean. And now, it looks like they've succeeded! The whale is swimming away right now. What a wonderful sight!

JIM: Thank you, Robin. Well, there was an emotional reunion at Chicago's O'Hare Airport today, when Stacy Baxter from Seattle, Washington, met Alicia Carson of Northfield, Illinois. The two women are twin sisters, but they had never met. They were born forty-five years ago and were adopted by two separate families. Four years ago, Ms. Baxter found out she was a twin and began to try to find her sister. She finally found out Ms. Carson's name and address last month. Ms. Baxter called her sister, and the twins met for the first time today! Karen.

KAREN: And after this message, we'll tell you about tomorrow's weather.

2 Listen again 📼

1. Have students begin by reading the summaries and trying to guess the missing words before they listen to the news reports. By previewing the stories, they'll find it easier to understand the recorded material.

2. Pause the tape after each news report so that students have time to work. You may want them to compare answers with a partner after each report.

Answers
1. winds, flames, families, control
2. rescued, hospital, operation, success
3. ocean, scared, guide
4. twin, separated, adopted

3 Group work

Have students form groups of three or four to compare their answers. All the endings were happy, so there may be some disagreement about which one is the happiest!

1 Pair work

1. Form an even number of pairs, and display a large wall map of the world if one is available. If your students are unaware of what's happening in the world, it may be best to do this as a whole-class brainstorming activity. You should prepare yourself by looking through a newspaper for ideas.

2. In a multinational class, you may want to avoid any conflict between antagonistic nationalities by asking everyone to focus on *good* news, not wars and conflicts.

3. Go around the class, prompting students who are stuck by mentioning events and countries that have been in the news recently.

2 Join another pair

Have students compare ideas.

Before the next lesson

Make sure that everyone notices the instructions on the bottom of page 47. Have students find one or two amusing or interesting short news items from a newspaper. They will need these in order to successfully do Activity D in the next lesson. If there's a local English-language newspaper, they should use it. If not, the article can be from a newspaper in their own language – the gist of which they'll have to communicate to the rest of the class in English, of course.

Follow-up activity

If you think your students have a fairly good grasp of world affairs, ask them to look at the map of the world and think of one *trouble spot* on each continent. Ask questions to facilitate discussion. For example: "Which countries were last year's trouble spots?" (Students should think of wars that were going on, disasters that happened, or violent events that occurred.) "In which of those countries has the situation improved since last year? Are they still in the news?"

To help students think of trouble spots, present a suitable example to start them off – preferably a situation that has improved since last year. Again, be careful not to discuss sensitive issues that may antagonize students.

Writing activity

Give students the following directions for a writing task:

Cut out a photo from a newspaper or magazine and write the story behind it. Tell the story from the point of view of a person in the photo or from the point of view of the person who took the photo.

22 Keep up to date!

Activity A

page 48

Vocabulary

newsmagazine   a weekly magazine that reports on the news, such as *Newsweek* or *Time*
comics   a section of the newspaper with stories that are told in pictures
controversial   causing disagreement and discussion
upset   unhappy
strong feelings   powerful emotions that somebody has about something

1 Work alone

Have students complete Activity A1 at home before coming to class, or have them complete it in class working alone. Circulate around the class offering assistance as necessary.

2 Group work

Divide the class into groups of three or four, and point out the expressions in the speech balloon. Give students some time to discuss their answers.

Activity B

page 49

Vocabulary

briefcase   a bag used to carry documents
to applaud   to show approval by clapping one's hands together
honeymoon   the vacation a couple takes after their wedding
off the hook   without replacing the receiver
to crawl   to move about on one's hands and knees
rattle   a small toy that makes a noise when you shake it
challenge   a difficult job
to attempt   to try
on board   on a train, ship, or airplane
a ferry   a boat that carries people short distances

1 Read/listen 📼

1. Ask students to read the articles and guess the missing words before coming to class. If it is not possible to assign the reading for homework, allow plenty of class time for students to complete the task working in pairs.

2. Play the tape, pausing after each article so that students have time to write their answers. You might also want them to compare answers with a partner after each report.

3. Discuss other plausible answers (for example, *sounds* for *noise* in the first article).

see next page for transcript

Transcript and answers   3 minutes

Missing words are in bold type.

Walkman Revenge

A **train** commuter in England was so angry at the **noise** coming from a young man's Walkman that he took a pair of scissors from his **briefcase** and cut through the headphone wire. His fellow **passengers** applauded.

Time Is Money

A woman in Chicago was very **angry** when her ex-husband remarried. While he and his new wife were on their **honeymoon**, she broke into his apartment and **telephoned** the "speaking clock" in London for the time. She left the phone off the hook and went home. The phone was off the hook until the **couple** got back from vacation two weeks later. The phone **bill** came to over eight thousand dollars.

Virtual Baby

For people who like **children** but don't have the time for a family, Quality Video of Minneapolis, Minnesota, U.S.A., has **produced** "Video Baby." This thirty-minute tape shows two babies doing what babies do, like crawl around the house, **play** with a rattle, take a bubble bath, and turn **lunch** into a complete mess. There's no narrator, so once the **tape** is in the VCR, there's nothing to come between the viewer and the baby but the **Off** button.

Of course, some things are left out, like babies **crying** and spitting up, not to mention the **challenge** of a full diaper. As the package says, "Enjoy bath time without being **splashed**, mealtime without wearing the food." Sound good? Imagine the possibilities for "Video Teenager."

Free Trip to the U.S.

Two Irish boys went to New York last week after their mothers told them not to play far from home because **dinner** was almost ready. They traveled without **tickets** from Dublin to London – and then on to New York's Kennedy Airport.

Noel Murray, aged thirteen, and Keith Byrne, ten, were picked up by the **police** outside Kennedy Airport because they looked "tired and **dirty**."

The youths were flown **home** to their parents yesterday. Keith's mother, Teresa, said to reporters: "I told him not to go far."

"We didn't really **know** what we wanted to do when we got there," Keith said last night. "We got off the **plane** with the other people, but we didn't see much of New York."

The trip is the boys' second **attempt** to see the world this month. Two weeks ago they were caught on board a **ferry** to England and sent home to their parents.

2 Join a partner

Form an even number of pairs for this discussion.

3 Pair work

Have students work with the same partner to compose summaries of each story. Go around helping as necessary. The sample answers are just suggestions.

Sample answers

This story is about . . .

1. a train passenger who was annoyed by someone's noisy Walkman.
2. a woman who left her ex-husband's phone off the hook in revenge.
3. a video of a baby for people who don't want a real baby.
4. two boys who managed to travel from Dublin to New York without tickets.

4 Join another pair

1. Have the groups compare their answers to the questions in Activity B2 as well as their summaries.
2. Ask various students to read aloud their best summaries.

Activity C

page 50

Vocabulary

eyewitness   a person who has seen an event and can describe it later (often in court)

Pair work

1. Have students discuss the questions. This is a warm-up for Activities D and E.
2. You may want to have a brief discussion before moving on to Activity D.

Activity D

page 50

Group work

Have students form groups and talk about their articles. Postpone this activity until the next class period if students haven't remembered to bring their articles (notes on this activity are under the "Before the next lesson" section of Lesson 21, Activity C).

Activity E

page 50

Communication task

Vocabulary

reliable   dependable; trustworthy
bench   a long, wooden seat, usually found in a park
sidewalk   a path next to a road for people to walk on

Procedure

1. Be sure to look at the photo on page 50 and Task 25 on page C-15 before the lesson so that you can answer any questions that may arise.
2. Divide students into an even number of pairs.
3. Review the directions with students. Emphasize that for this activity to work, they must look at the photo on page 50 *before* turning to Task 25 on page C-15. Also, once they turn to the task, they *must not* look back at the photo. Tell everyone that this is a game to test their memories.
4. Have everyone look at the photo for 10 seconds only and turn to Task 25.
5. When they've discussed all the questions, have two pairs join together and compare their answers. They should still not look at page 50.
6. Reassemble the class and allow everyone to look at the photo on page 50 again. Ask for comments and reactions. Did anyone get all the answers right?

Writing activity

Give students the following directions for a writing task:

Write a report or a story about the events leading up to and following the moment the photo on page 50 was taken.

Review puzzles

page 51

The vocabulary in Puzzle A is from Lessons 17–20. The vocabulary in Puzzle B is from Lessons 21–22.

Puzzle A

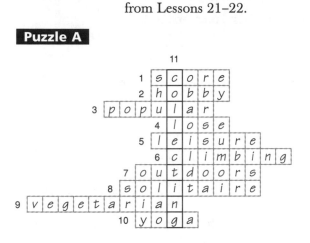

11

1 s c o r e
2 h o b b y
3 p o p u l a r
4 l o s e
5 l e i s u r e
6 c l i m b i n g
7 o u t d o o r s
8 s o l i t a i r e
9 v e g e t a r i a n
10 y o g a

Puzzle B

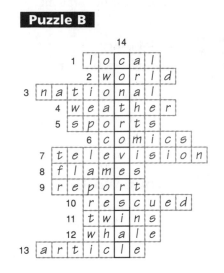

14

1 l o c a l
2 w o r l d
3 n a t i o n a l
4 w e a t h e r
5 s p o r t s
6 c o m i c s
7 t e l e v i s i o n
8 f l a m e s
9 r e p o r t
10 r e s c u e d
11 t w i n s
12 w h a l e
13 a r t i c l e

23 City life

Unit 11, *Living in the city*, consists of Lessons 23–24. It focuses on cities of the world, the advantages of city and country life, and crime.

Activity A

page 52

Vocabulary

middle-aged   being between, approximately, forty and sixty years old
gorgeous   wonderful; beautiful
the holidays   a time when there are public holidays and people are off from work

1 Pair work

1. Ask the class if they like where they live. Find out what they like and dislike about city or country life. Then divide students into pairs.

2. As pairs talk about the photos, move around the class assisting with vocabulary as necessary.

3. Reassemble the class and have students take turns describing the photos. Then ask questions such as the following: "Which of the photos could have been taken in your city? What cities do you think are shown?"

Answers

the jazz club: New Orleans, Louisiana, U.S.A.
the park: Union Square park, New York City, New York, U.S.A.
the outdoor restaurants: Boogis St., Singapore
the train: Tokyo, Japan

2 Listen 📻

Play the tape. You may have to pause it occasionally to give everyone enough time to work. Tell students not to worry if they didn't get *all* the advantages mentioned on the tape.

Answers

Advantages of city life (Jeffrey)	Advantages of country life (Kevin)
interesting, very good jobs	quieter
museums	air is better
movies	more relaxed
concerts	not crowded with tourists
theaters	gorgeous
fun	

see next page for transcript

Transcript   1 minute 30 seconds

KEVIN: Hello.

JEFFREY: Hey, Kevin. It's Jeffrey. I bet you know why I'm calling, huh?

KEVIN: Yeah, I guess so. L-look, I haven't changed my mind.

JEFFREY: OK, well, the room is still free. But . . . uh . . . not for much longer. I mean, I have to find someone else to move in here if you don't want to do it.

KEVIN: Oh, look, you know how I feel about moving to the city.

JEFFREY: Yeah, but on the other hand, you did say you were looking for a new job, and there are plenty of interesting and very good jobs in the city.

KEVIN: If you say so.

JEFFREY: Mmm. Just think of all the great museums, right? (Hmm.) The wonderful movies, and you got concerts, you got theaters –

KEVIN: I know, I know, I know. Well, you know, it's just . . . it's much quieter out here, and, you know, the air is j-just better out here. I-I don't know, life is just – it's more relaxed.

JEFFREY: You sound like you're getting middle-aged.

KEVIN: No, no, no, I don't think that's fair. I mean, you know how the city is at this time of the year, especially with all the tourists, I mean. And you know how gorgeous it is out here, right?

JEFFREY: Yeah, I guess so, but living in the city can be a lot of fun. Listen, why don't you just come and stay with me once more, say, over the holidays, and we can talk about it some more?

KEVIN: Huh. . . . Uh, you know, that could be fun.

3 Join a partner

1. Have students form pairs and compare their notes from the previous activity before they move on to the discussion questions. As they talk, they should take notes on more advantages of city and country life. Also ask students to write down the two words they would use to describe the city or town where they live.

2. Reassemble the class and ask students to report on the advantages that they noted. Then have students tell the class the two words they selected, and why they chose them.

Sample answers

Other advantages might include the following:

City life	Country life
stores	less crime
restaurants	usually cheaper
bars and cafés	traffic is less heavy
clubs	closer to nature

Follow-up activity

Ask students what things they can find in a city that they aren't as likely to find in a small town. Give them a few examples such as the following: movie theaters, restaurants, a large university, traffic jams, violence, crime. Brainstorm a list of ideas on the board. Here are some ideas they might come up with: *museums, high schools, offices, skyscrapers, high-rise buildings, cathedrals, parks, department stores, zoos, shopping malls, churches or temples, subways, buses, expressways, commuters, murders, robberies, drugs, pickpockets, pollution, homelessness.*

If you'd like students to categorize the items, create three columns as you write the ideas on the board. List the things that are "bad" in the right-hand column, the ones that are "good" in the left-hand column, and the things that are neutral in the center column. Have students tell you where to place each item as it is called out.

Activity B

page 53

Vocabulary

urban   belonging to a city (not a small town)
inhabitant   a person who lives in a particular place

1 Pair work

1. Divide the class into an even number of pairs. Remind students that the population figures given refer to contiguous urban areas (i.e., Yokohama is included under Tokyo; the population of Osaka includes the cities of Kobe and Kyoto).

2. Circulate around the class as students interpret the bar charts and find the answers to the first four questions. Students can talk about the fifth question with their partner, or discuss it as a class.

Answers

1. Lagos
2. Osaka, London
3. 12
4. South Asia (Bombay, Dhaka), Africa (Lagos)

2 Group work

1. Combine pairs into groups of four for this discussion.

2. After the discussion, take a class poll to find out which city your students would most like to live in.

3. If there's time, ask the class if they know which country each of the cities is in.

Answers

Tokyo, Japan	Seoul, South Korea	Paris, France
New York, U.S.A.	Jakarta, Indonesia	Cairo, Egypt
São Paulo, Brazil	Buenos Aires, Argentina	Moscow, Russia
Mexico City, Mexico	Osaka, Japan	Manila, the Philippines
Shanghai, China	Tianjin, China	Istanbul, Turkey
Bombay, India	Rio de Janeiro, Brazil	Dhaka, Bangladesh
Los Angeles, U.S.A.	Lagos, Nigeria	London, England
Beijing, China	Delhi, India	
Calcutta, India	Karachi, Pakistan	

Communication task

page 53

Vocabulary

carving   a figure made by cutting wood into a special shape
sourdough   a special mixture of flour and water used to make bread
architecture   the style of a building
shopping mall   a place where many stores are gathered together in one area, often covered by a roof
artifact   an object of historical interest

Procedure

1. Be sure to look at the two tasks (Task 23 on page C-14 and Task 31 on page C-18) before the lesson so that you can answer any questions that may arise. Students will exchange information about Seoul/Venice and San Francisco/Rio de Janeiro. The information for each task covers an entire page, so you may need extra time for this activity. You can simplify the activity by having four students – two students per page – work together.

2. Divide students into pairs and tell them which tasks to look at. Tell them not to worry about pronouncing the Portuguese, Korean, or Italian words correctly.

3. Go around the class, helping as necessary.

4. Reassemble the class and find out which city was the most popular and why. If students in the class have actually visited any of these places, ask them if they think the information presented about the place(s) was accurate and if they can provide any additional information of their own.

Writing activity

Give students the following directions for a writing task:

Choose one of these writing tasks:

Describe your favorite city and explain why you like it.
Describe a city you don't like and explain why you dislike it.

24 Safety and crime

Activity A

page 54

Vocabulary

personal alarm a small gadget you can use to make a loud noise if you are attacked

1 Work alone
Have students complete the questionnaire.

2 Join a partner
Ask students to join a partner and compare answers.

Activity B

pages 54–55

Vocabulary

to buzz in to let someone into your apartment building by pressing a button that is in your apartment
roommate a person who shares a rented apartment or house with another person
platform the part of a station where you stand while waiting for a train or subway
subway conductor the person on a subway who calls out subway stops to passengers and opens and closes the subway doors

1 Listen

Play the tape, pausing after each speaker. The students may need to hear the tape twice to get all the answers.

Answers

Who . . . ?	Larry	Anne	Paul
stands near other people while waiting for the subway		✔	
has locks on the windows of his/her apartment	✔		
avoids making eye contact with people on the street			✔
has his/her apartment keys ready		✔	
doesn't walk alone late at night	✔		
doesn't let strangers into his/her apartment building	✔		
rides in the subway car with the conductor late at night			✔
always looks like he/she knows where he/she's going			✔
always tells his/her roommate where he/she's going		✔	

see next page for transcript

Transcript   2 minutes 10 seconds

First, Larry.

INTERVIEWER: You live in the city. (Mm-hmm.) Do you feel safe there?

LARRY: Well, I would say that I do feel safe. But . . . uh . . . then, of course, I take precautions. I think you have to if you live in the city. For instance, inside my apartment . . . uh . . . my front door has several locks on it. And on all the windows I have locks, too. And that's something maybe not everyone does, but . . . uh . . . it certainly helps keep burglars away. You would hear them if they were trying to break in . . . uh . . . with a lock on the window.

Um . . . At the front door of the building, I don't let anybody into the building through the front door if I don't know them. Uh . . . If they're strangers asking to be, you know, buzzed in, I won't let them in.

And in my neighborhood, . . . uh . . . I don't walk alone at night. If it's late at night, I won't . . . uh . . . won't walk on the streets alone, especially if it's a really dark, quiet street. No way.

Now, Anne.

ANNE: Well, let's see, what do I do to be safe? Well, one thing I do to be safe is I always tell someone exactly where I'm going, usually my roommate. So somebody knows where I am at all times.

And another thing is: When I come home late at night, I always have my keys ready at the front door, so I don't have to stop there and look for my keys in my purse.

Oh, and one more thing I do is when I'm on the subway platform, I always am sure to stand near other people. I don't like to be standing alone on the subway platform.

Finally, Paul.

PAUL: Let's see, what do I do to be safe? Well, when I ride the subway late at night, I always try to ride in the car with the conductor.

And if I'm on the subway, or even walking down the street, I never stare at anyone. You know, I . . . I avoid making direct eye contact.

Oh, and I . . . I always try to look like I know where I'm going. I move very quickly, walk quickly.

2 Join a partner

Arrange students into an even number of pairs to compare answers and discuss the safety precautions. The speakers in the recording live in New York City. If your students live in a relatively safe place, they may think some of the precautions the speakers mention sound rather bizarre.

3 Group work

Have students form groups and discuss the questions.

Vocabulary

injury   damage to a person's body
car thefts   number of cars that are stolen
graffiti   funny, rude, or political writings on walls and doors in public places

1 Pair work

Arrange the class into an even number of pairs. Ask students to interpret the statistics presented in the chart. For example, "The most murders happen in the United States." "The most road accident injuries happen in Germany." If statistics for your students' countries are not included in the chart, try to find the information in a resource book before coming to class.

2 Group work

1. Combine pairs into groups for this activity. There are no "correct answers" – some students may consider all the situations to be serious crimes.

2. Reassemble the class and find out which situations the groups ranked 1 (the most serious) and 8 (the least serious) and why.

3. Optional discussion idea: Ask students how they think the situations should be resolved (through punishment or by other means). Students could also tell the class what they would say to a friend who had committed one of these "crimes."

4. Ask students what they would do if they found the following things on the sidewalk:

a wallet containing money	a fifty-dollar bill
a ten-dollar bill	a nice pen
a glove	a bunch of keys

Writing activity

Give students the following directions for a writing task:

Write a letter to a friend overseas who's coming to visit you in your country. Tell your friend what to do to remain safe during his or her stay.

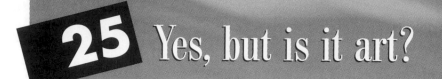

25 Yes, but is it art?

Unit 12, *Arts and entertainment*, consists of Lessons 25–26.

Activity A

pages 56–57

Vocabulary

horizontal   flat and level; parallel to the ground
vertical   standing or pointing straight up from the ground

1 Pair work

1. Start by telling the class that they don't have to know about art to participate in this activity.

2. Divide students into an even number of pairs and give them time to talk about the pictures.

2 Join another pair

1. Combine pairs into groups of four for the discussion.

2. Reassemble the class and ask students to tell you who their favorite artists are.

3 Class activity

Have students read about the artists and match them to their paintings. This activity will give students who are knowledgeable about art a chance to show their expertise. Let the discussion continue for as long as you feel appropriate.

Answers

clockwise from upper left-hand corner

flower: Georgia O'Keeffe
sculpture of torso: Fernando Botero
landscape: Nicolas Poussin

two women: Frida Kahlo
abstract painting: Piet Mondrian
horse: Xu Beihong

Activity B

page 57

Vocabulary

pottery   clay objects made by hand, such as vases or bowls
circumstances   a situation; a set of conditions

Group work

1. Arrange the class into groups of three or four. These questions are philosophical in nature so there are no correct answers.

2. Reassemble the class after the discussions are finished and ask various students to share their opinions with the class. Your students may be eager to hear what you think, but don't tell them your views until the very end.

Communication task

Procedure

1. Be sure to look at Task 27 on page C-16 before the lesson so that you can answer any questions that may arise. There is some difficult vocabulary here!

2. Divide the class into an even number of pairs and ask them to look at Task 27. Review the words in the vocabulary box.

3. Make sure that students understand the procedure: First one student guesses which painting his or her partner has described and then they switch roles.

4. Have pairs form groups of four and discuss the questions.

5. Reassemble the class and ask students from each group to report on the conclusions they reached.

The three pictures in Task 27 (from left to right) are:

American Gothic by Grant Wood
Bride and Groom by Amedeo Modigliani
The Arnolfini Marriage by Jan Van Eyck

Follow-up activity

Ask everyone to bring to class a postcard (or a reproduction in a book) of a favorite painting. Tell students to plan on explaining why they bought the card (and what memories it brings back to them) and why they like the painting. Bring in any postcards that you may have and demonstrate to the class how they might talk about their cards by telling them about yours. Have students discuss the postcards in small groups.

Writing activity

Give students the following directions for a writing task:
Describe your favorite painting and why you like it.

26 I really enjoyed it!

Activity A

page 58

Vocabulary

> **ballet**   a performance by dancers to music without words, such as *Swan Lake*
> **symphony**   a concert by a symphony orchestra
> **play**   a nonmusical performance on a stage, such as *Hamlet* or *Romeo and Juliet*

1 Pair work

Arrange the class into pairs to discuss the photos. Students will find it easy enough to put the events in order of preference, but may find it more challenging to explain their reasons.

2 Pair work

Rearrange pairs so that each student is working with someone he or she doesn't know well. Have students ask their partners questions to complete the questionnaire.

3 Class activity

Reassemble the class for this activity. Have students report how they and their partners have similar/different tastes.

Activity B

page 59

Vocabulary

> **hilarious**   very funny
> **offensive**   disgusting

1 Pair work

1. Have students work together to complete the chart and add two words to their list.
2. Reassemble the class and make a list of the two new words on the board.

Answers

Positive words	Negative words
exciting, hilarious, thrilling, brilliant, funny, clever	terrible, awful, horrible, disappointing, violent, offensive
Possible additional words moving, amusing, beautiful, wonderful, excellent	*Possible additional words* frightening, dull, boring, dreadful, stupid, silly

94 | Arts and entertainment

2 Read/listen 📼

1. Have students read the movie review and try to guess the missing words. (To save time this could be done as homework before the lesson.)
2. Play the tape, pausing after each paragraph to give students time to work.

Transcript and answers   1 minute 25 seconds

Missing words are in bold type.

Meet the Applegates

The Applegates are a clean-living, model American **family**. Father Dick is a security man at a power plant. Mother Jane is a housewife. **Teenagers** Sally and Johnny are great kids. But what no one knows is that the Applegates are really **insects**! They come from the Amazon rain **forest** and have disguised themselves as humans so that they can start a campaign to stop people from **destroying** their home.

While they're **planning** their campaign, the Applegates try to make friends and act like a normal family (which isn't easy since they only eat **garbage** and liquid sugar!). But they soon have **problems**. Jane starts charging too much on her new **credit** cards, and Johnny becomes friends with a **wild** crowd of heavy-metal fans. Sally gets pregnant, and Dick falls in love with another woman. But thankfully Aunt Bea Applegate arrives to **save** the day!

Packed with **clever** special effects, witty observations, and plenty of **humor**, *Meet the Applegates* is a **funny** film with an environmental theme.

3 Join a partner

1. Arrange the class into an even number of pairs. Have students discuss their reasons.
2. After students have finished their discussions, you may want to state your opinion of the movie so that the students can compare their reasons with yours.

4 Group work

1. Combine pairs into groups to discuss the questions.
2. Reassemble the class and have students report their findings to the class.

Follow-up activity

If there are lots of movie buffs in your class, here are some extra questions they might like to discuss as a class or in small groups:

What is the most frightening movie you've ever seen? Why was it so frightening?
What is the most moving movie you've ever seen? Why was it so moving?
What is the most exciting movie you've ever seen? Why was it so exciting?
What was the worst movie you've ever seen? Why was it so bad?

Tell students that if a classmate talks about a movie they haven't seen, they should ask the student to briefly describe the plot of the movie.

(Note: Funny movies will be discussed again in Lesson 29.)

Activity C

page 60

Vocabulary

tune   a melody
easy listening   music that is soft and melodic
heavy metal   rock music with loud electric guitars
musical taste   the kind of music a person chooses to listen to
instrument   an object that makes music, such as a piano or guitar

1 Listen

Have students listen to the music and decide which style they like the most. Each piece of music is recorded twice on the tape.

Time   1 minute

The music on the tape is:

1. classical
2. jazz
3. heavy metal
4. country and western
5. easy listening

2 Listen again

Have students listen again and identify each musical style.

Answers

country and western, 4;   jazz, 2;   classical, 1;   easy listening, 5;   heavy metal, 3

3 Join a partner

1. Form an even number of pairs. Talking about music is quite difficult, but everyone should be able to talk about their tastes in music and say what kinds of music they like.

2. Reassemble the class and brainstorm the names of some other musical instruments (for example, *trumpet, electric guitar, clarinet, cello*).

Answers

Additional kinds of music: folk, gospel, choral, opera, reggae, salsa

Names of the instruments (from left to right): violin, saxophone, (grand) piano, flute, drum, guitar

4 Join another pair

Combine pairs and allow students plenty of time to discuss the questions. Be prepared for long discussions.

Writing activity

Give students the following directions for a writing task:

Write a review of a movie you've seen recently or a review of your favorite film.

Review puzzles

page 61

The vocabulary in Puzzle A is from Lessons 23–24. The vocabulary in Puzzle B is from Lessons 25–26.

Puzzle A

Puzzle B

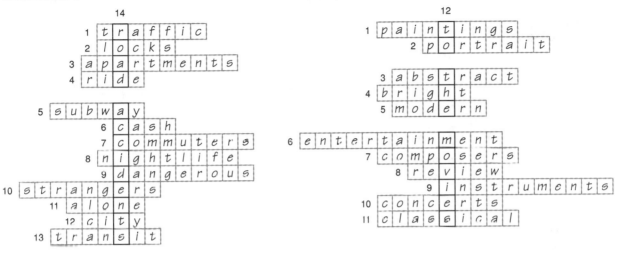

Times have changed

Unit 13, *In the past*, consists of Lessons 27–28. It focuses on memories of childhood, reminiscences, and historic places.

Activity A

page 62

1 Pair work

Divide the class into an even number of pairs. Review the expression *What is he like?* (students may confuse this with *What does he like?*). Students will need to examine the photos carefully to answer the questions. There are no right answers to these questions.

2 Join another pair

1. Have students continue the discussion in groups of four.
2. If there's time, ask students what their desks would show about their own interests.

Activity B

page 63

Vocabulary

bunk beds   two beds on top of each other, as in a ship
comic book   a book with stories told in pictures
to spoil   to give a child too much praise and attention, so that he or she becomes selfish
tag, hopscotch, jump rope   children's games
responsibilities   required duties, such as paying bills
creepy   frightening; giving an unpleasant feeling
security guard   a person who makes sure a building is secure at night
date   an appointment to go to a social event, often made between a man and a woman
pal   a friend
league   a group of teams that have joined together to play sports
Little League baseball   a baseball league for children aged eight to twelve
pretending   behaving as if something is true when you know it is not really true
to appreciate   to be thankful for

1 Listen 📟

1. Play the tape, pausing after each speaker. Students may need to hear the tape twice to get all the answers.
2. Play the tape a third time, so that students can *enjoy* the stories without having a task to worry about. Pause between each speaker to answer any questions, and replay any segments of the conversation students would like to hear again.

Answers

Who. . . ?	Phil	Wanda	Tom
hid in the museum with his/her girlfriend		✔	
liked being treated as a friend by his/her father			✔
loved comic books	✔		
loved making up stories		✔	
loved playing games		✔	
loved sports			✔
slept in the same room as his/her brother and sisters	✔		
was spoiled because he/she was the youngest	✔		
went on his/her first date			✔

Transcript 4 minutes

Phil.

INTERVIEWER: Phil, what do you remember about being twelve years old?

PHIL: Well, when I was twelve years old, my p– family was very poor, and we lived in this tiny apartment downtown with . . . uh . . . three older sisters and one older brother, and we all slept in the same bedroom on bunk beds.

I was a big collector of comic books when I was twelve. I used to collect all the Superman and Batman comic books, used to run to the store every Thursday when they came out, and they'd cost about ten cents back then. And all the friends would get together, and we'd go to the corner store and buy comic books, and then head back for the playground and spend the next hour reading comics and . . . and exchanging them and . . . and just talking about them.

INTERVIEWER: So what was the best thing about being twelve?

PHIL: Well, my mother would spoil me because I was the baby, and I would always get more toys than they ever did. I would also get to eat whatever I wanted to. Um . . . It was also a time when I knew that if I got into any kind of trouble . . . uh . . . in the neighborhood that my older sisters and my brother would come and protect me.

Wanda.

INTERVIEWER: Tell us what you remember about when you were twelve years old.

WANDA: I remember . . . um . . . playing endlessly. I used to love to play tag and hopscotch and jump rope, double Dutch, chase boys. The best thing about being twelve was being carefree and not really having any responsibilities, having lots of friends, and playing. I loved to tell stories – I loved to make up stories and act them out, and play dress-up – that was always a lot of fun.

INTERVIEWER: Do you remember any special things that happened to you the year you were twelve?

transcript continues on next page

Activity B

*page 63
continued*

WANDA: Yeah. Me and my girlfriend decided that we wanted to sleep in the museum one night to see if, like, any of the exhibits moved. So we . . . um . . . we hid behind a wall, and the . . . the museum closed, and it was really creepy because it was, like, eight o'clock at night, and we could just hear footsteps around. We didn't know it was the security guard, and we got really scared and gave ourselves up, and that was . . . that was a good memory.

Tom.

INTERVIEWER: Tell us what you remember about being twelve years old.

TOM: Uh . . . Twelve years old. Uh . . . Let's see, that was probably . . . uh . . . my first interest in girls, my first . . . uh . . . uh . . . "date," so to speak. Uh . . . I went to a dance – I think it was a sixth-grade dance with this girl. My mom . . . uh . . . you know, drove me over to her house, and I got out of the car, and, you know, greeted her, and brought her to the dance. It was . . . uh – I guess it was my first date, really.

INTERVIEWER: What was the best thing about being twelve years old?

TOM: Uh . . . The best thing . . . the best thing probably was . . . um . . . uh . . . the relationship with my father started to . . . to change a little. Um . . . He started to . . . uh . . . not take more of an interest, but he started to sort of . . . uh . . . treat me differently, you know. He would . . . he would call me "pal," you know, instead of "son." And . . . uh . . . I think he started to try to act more like a friend. I mean, I know he was, you know, pretending . . . uh . . . that that change was happening, but . . . uh . . . you know, I . . . I appreciated it, you know. (Mm-hmm.) When I was twelve, I was much more athletic than I am now. You know, I was . . . uh . . . involved in all sorts of sports – uh . . . Little League baseball and . . . um . . . basketball, and I even played some football. You know, . . . uh . . . had a lot of great moments. Yeah, glory days, you know.

2 Listen

Vocabulary

rent   the money you pay to the owner of the apartment you live in
candy   sweet snacks made from sugar
commitment   something you have promised you will do

1. Play the tape twice (first for students to get the gist, and again for the details). Tell students that they don't need to write down all the differences. Expect them to catch one or two differences.

2. Check answers as a class. If most students found the tape difficult, you might play it a third time before the discussion in Activity B3 begins.

Answers

Tom	doesn't really feel it's that different
	doesn't think differently now
Phil	fewer responsibilities then
	didn't have to pay rent
	could spend all his time eating candy, reading comic books, watching TV

Wanda no bills, responsibilities, or commitments
could be carefree
endless free time for playing
opportunity to dream and pretend you can be whatever you want to be

Transcript   1 minute 30 seconds

First, Tom.

INTERVIEWER: How was your life different then from the way it is now?

TOM: Uh . . . You know, I don't . . . I don't really think it's that different, actually. Um . . . I mean, I know it is, but . . . uh . . . as far . . . as far as in my head or the way I feel or the way I think, I don't . . . I don't feel that different, you know. I don't think that differently.

Now, Phil.

PHIL: I did like the fact that there were fewer responsibilities when I was twelve. I didn't have rent to pay, and I could spend all my time eating candy and reading

comic books and watching a lot of television.

Finally, Wanda.

WANDA: Well, . . . now I have bills and responsibilities and commitments, and, like I said, back when I was twelve years old, it just seemed like there was just endless amounts of time for playing, and I had no responsibilities, and I just could be carefree. There's a certain kind of lightness about being twelve, and youth, and . . . just the world is yours, and you just have an opportunity to dream and pretend that you can be whatever you want to be.

3 Join a partner

1. Have students compare answers and discuss the questions. If they can't remember anything significant about when they were twelve, encourage them to talk about their childhoods in general.

2. Reassemble the class to find out how many people would like to be twelve again, and why they feel the way they do.

Activity C

page 63

Communication task 🗣️🗣️

Vocabulary

to figure out   to work out the answer
to reminisce   to talk about things you remember happening in the past

Procedure

1. Be sure to look at the two tasks (Task 21 on page C-13 and Task 32 on page C-19) before the lesson so that you can answer any questions that may arise.

2. Arrange the class into groups of four. Have two students look at Task 21 while two students look at Task 32.

3. Have each pair prepare a story from the scenes in their books. After the story has been completed, have the students reminisce about what happened, with each student taking on the role of one of the characters in their story. Point out the language in the speech balloon.

procedure continues on next page

Activity C

page 63
continued

4. Split pairs up and have each student from Task 21 compare his or her story with a new partner from Task 32. There's one scene in common between the stories in the two tasks. Let students discover this for themselves in due course.

Writing activity

Give students the following directions for a writing task:

Write about a great day out that you remember. Describe what you did and tell why it was such an enjoyable day.

28 A sense of history

This lesson focuses on historic places and on important historical events. Students may need to do some preparation before attempting Activity B2 and Activity C.

Activity A
pages 64–65

Vocabulary

historic important in history
shrine a kind of temple or place of worship
veranda a long balcony
to decline to become less in number or importance
abandoned left alone
ruins remains of a building after it has fallen or burnt down
ancient very old
monument a building or statue put up in memory of someone or some event
pillar a strong column made of stone
horseshoe pattern in the shape of the letter U
observatory a place where you watch the stars
fence a kind of wall made of wood

1 Pair work

Tell students that this activity is a warm-up for Activity A2. They should look at the pictures and discuss the questions.

2 Read/listen

1. Have students try to guess the missing words. They can work in pairs or alone.
2. Play the tape, pausing after each description. You may want to have students compare their answers with a partner.

Transcript and answers   2 minutes 15 seconds

Missing words are in bold type.

Kiyomizu

During the period from 794 to 1868, when Kyoto was the capital of Japan, over 2,000 Buddhist temples and Shinto **shrines** were built in the city. One beautiful **temple** is named Kiyomizu. Built in 1633, the present buildings of Kiyomizu are set high on a **hill**.

As you walk up the hill, you can see the **roofs** of the temple buildings rising above one another. From the veranda of the largest **building**, you can look across the city of Kyoto.

transcript continues on next page

Activity A

pages 64–65 continued

Teotihuacán

Two thousand years ago, Teotihuacán, located north of Mexico City, was the largest **city** in the Americas, the capital of a powerful state of 100,000 inhabitants. It began to decline after 600 A.D. and was eventually abandoned and burned. When the Aztecs discovered the **ruins** years later, they believed the city had been **built** by gods. Visitors can **walk** along the Avenue of the Dead to the enormous Temple of the Sun, from which there is a **view** of the ruined city. Every evening a sound and light show tells the story of the **ancient** city and its people.

Stonehenge

Scientists estimate that Stonehenge, a **monument** in Wiltshire, England, dates from 2000 B.C., but nobody knows why it was built. It consists of a circle of 30 upright stone pillars connected with flat **stones** laid across the top. Within the circle are five big stones in a horseshoe pattern and one pillar that faces the **sun**. Because of this, some people think Stonehenge was an ancient observatory. Others, however, believe it was a temple and **burial** ground. Although **visitors** can't touch the stones, they can view them from behind a fence.

3 Join a partner

Have students compare their answers.

4 Pair work

Ask students to work in pairs to answer the questions. Students might enjoy learning that in Japanese the expression "to jump from the Kiyomizu veranda" means to do something daring and irrevocable.

Answers

1. from the veranda of the largest building at Kiyomizu and from the Temple of the Sun at Teotihuacán
2. all of them (although not all experts agree that Stonehenge was a temple)
3. Teotihuacán and Stonehenge

Activity B

page 65

Vocabulary

site   a place; a location

1 Pair work

1. Have students look at the silhouettes of buildings in the picture. Discuss what kind of building each one is. The silhouettes are deliberately ambiguous: From left to right they show a cathedral or church, temple or parliament, tower or skyscraper, palace or mosque, and a castle or gateway. This discussion will be particularly helpful if students' cities or regions don't have any sites as ancient or famous as the ones in Activity A.

2. Form pairs for the discussion. There's a lot to talk about here, so you may want to limit the discussion time.

3. Reassemble the class and find out which period in history students would have liked to live in and why.

104 | In the past

Copyright © Cambridge University Press

2 Work alone

Have students answer the two questions. You may have to brainstorm a list of historic sites and buildings as a class if students are having trouble coming up with answers individually. If you have a multinational class, you may want to focus on places that are close to the city students are studying in, rather than discussing a worldwide range of sites.

3 Join a partner

Have students do the role-play with a partner different from the one they worked with for Activity B1. Encourage the "visitor" to ask questions during the conversation.

Activity C

page 65

1 Pair work

Arrange the class into groups of four and then split the groups into pairs. In a multinational class, try to arrange students so that each group consists of more than one nationality. This is an opportunity to learn about the history of other countries.

2 Join another pair

1. Have students compare ideas and decide on the most significant event. In a multinational class, the students should decide on the most significant event in *each* country's history, rather than try to decide among the countries.

2. Reassemble the class to find out what the groups decided.

Writing activity

Give students the following directions for a writing task:

Write a description of a historic building or site in your region. Follow the same style as the descriptions on page 64.

29 What a scream!

Unit 14, *Comedy and humor*, consists of Lessons 29–30. It focuses on what makes people laugh, humor in different countries, and telling stories.

Activity A

pages 66–67

1 Pair work

Have students look at the scenes and discuss the questions. Young students may not be familiar with the movies or TV shows that these scenes came from, but it's the look of the scenes that they should respond to. They needn't describe the content of the shows in detail. Don't be too surprised if some students think that *none* of the scenes look funny.

Answers

Top row: Jim Carrey in *Ace Ventura, Pet Detective*; Lucille Ball in a scene from the TV show *I Love Lucy*. Bottom row: Charlie Chaplin in *City Lights*; Jerry Lewis in *The Nutty Professor*.

2 Pair work

1. Ask students to think of examples of humor from their own countries.
2. Reassemble the class to find out what extra words they added to the columns.

Answers

There is a lot of new vocabulary here, and some of the words may be difficult to define. You may want to limit the number of words you introduce to your students for this activity.

Types of humor	Funny people	Words for "funny"	Words for "laugh"
farce slapstick satire	cartoonist clown comedian	comical hilarious humorous	giggle snicker chuckle
Extra words that can be added:			
spoof cartoon parody black humor situation comedy joke pun	(practical) joker	silly	belly laugh

Vocabulary

comedy show   a program on TV that is supposed to make you laugh

1 Pair work

Form an even number of pairs. If students don't know the actors pictured, have them talk about their favorite comedy actors.

2 Join another pair

1. Combine pairs into groups of four for the discussion.
2. Reassemble the class and find out which questions provoked the most discussion. Find out about students' favorite actors and shows.

Communication task

Vocabulary

fancy dinner   an expensive dinner
goat   an animal with horns and a short tail

Procedure

1. Be sure to look at the three tasks (Task 22 on page C-13, Task 26 on page C-15, and Task 30 on page C-17) before the lesson so that you can answer any questions that may arise.
2. You may want to demonstrate how to tell a joke before the students begin the task. Here are some jokes to help you demonstrate.

> Dad, there's a lady at the door collecting for the new swimming pool!
>   Give her a glass of water.

> Doctor, Doctor, I feel like a dog.
>   Sit!

> Doctor, Doctor, everybody seems to ignore me.
>   Next patient, please!

> Waiter, there's a fly in my soup!
>   They just don't care what they eat, do they?

> Waiter, what's this fly doing in my soup?
>   Looks like he's trying to get out, sir.

3. Divide the class into groups of three. Each task contains two jokes. Make sure everyone tries to memorize their jokes before they tell them to their partners, rather than simply reading them aloud.
4. After all the jokes have been told, have students discuss which jokes they liked best. At this point, students can also try to think of more jokes to tell each other.

procedure continues on next page

Activity C

page 67
continued

5. Reassemble the class and tell them some more jokes:

> Waiter, your thumb is in my soup!
>> That's all right, sir. The soup isn't hot.

> I forgot my wife's birthday.
>> What did she say?
>
> Nothing . . . for five weeks.

> Who's that at the door?
>> The Invisible Man.
>
> Well, tell him I can't see him.

> Doctor, Doctor, I've lost my memory.
>> Oh, dear, when did this happen?
>
> When did what happen?

Writing activity

Give students the following directions for a writing task:

Write a joke or a funny story.

30 A sense of humor

Activity A

page 68

1 Pair work

Divide the class into an even number of pairs. Have students number the cartoons and answer the questions. Number the cartoons in order of funniness yourself, so that students can later compare their sense of humor with yours. Some students may not find the cartoons funny, and that should generate some discussion.

2 Join another pair

1. Combine pairs into groups of four. Have students compare their reactions and answer the questions. It *is* difficult to explain the point of a joke, but it's a good way of comparing different senses of humor.

2. Reassemble the class and find out which was the favorite cartoon, and tell the students how you ordered the cartoons.

Activity B

page 69

Vocabulary

clumsy   not careful
wire   a thin piece of metal
perch   a small swing for a bird to stand on
to pass out   to faint; to become unconscious
to come to   to become conscious again
Broadway show   a popular stage show in New York's theater district
to clean out   to take everything
trunk   the back part of a car that holds the spare tire and packages

1 Listen 📼

1. Play each of the stories. Pause the tape each time the bell is heard and ask students to guess what happened next.

2. Play the rest of the story so students can check their guesses. (Note: These stories are so-called urban myths – stories that people tell as if they happened to a friend of a friend, often in the sincere belief that they really happened. Interestingly, the same urban myths can be found in many countries around the world.)

Transcript   4 minutes 45 seconds

The three stories are recorded twice on the tape.

One.

MAN 1: My friend's grandmother called in some guys to fix this old gas stove in her kitchen. And they got there, and they started to work on the stove, and she decided she needed a few things from the store, so she l-l-left them alone to work.

Now these guys were really clumsy. They kept on dropping tools, and it was a wonder that the stove ever got fixed at all. And there was gas coming out of the pipe the whole time that they were

transcript continues on next page

working. But by the end they got it together, with only a couple of bolts left over.

And at that point one of them noticed a bird cage in the woman's living room. And there was a little bird on the floor of this cage with its legs up in the air – it was dead. Now they realized that there was going to be big trouble when this woman got back from the store and when she saw this gas had killed her poor, little bird. So these two guys, they take some wire, right, and they fix the dead bird upright on its perch. So they were b– ready to clear out of there, and they were just about to leave, when they heard a key in the lock.

This woman comes into her living room, she takes one look at the little bird's cage, and she just passed out. When she finally came to, she explained to them that it was quite a shock to see the little bird alive . . . because it had died earlier that morning!

Two.

WOMAN: I read in the paper about this couple from New Jersey. They woke up one morning to find their car missing from the driveway. So they called the police, and they reported it, and then they went to work.

And when they returned home from work, the car was back in the driveway with a note attached to the windshield wipers. And inside the envelope, the note said, "I'm sorry I had to borrow your car. My wife was pregnant, about to give birth to our baby. I don't have a car. It was an emergency. I needed to take her to the hospital. Please accept my apology." And he enclosed two tickets to a Broadway show.

So the couple thought, "OK, the car is back, tickets, apology." So on the weekend, they went to the show, and when they returned home, they discovered that someone had cleaned out

their entire house. They took everything. They thought, well, it must be the person who stole the car.

And they later found out that the car had been used in a robbery on the very same day that it disappeared.

Three.

MAN 2: My brother-in-law, he had the most amazing experience the other day. He was at the supermarket, and he's . . . uh . . . wheeling his groceries out to his car, and he starts unloading them into his trunk, and he's watching this woman a few cars down doing the same thing. And . . . only she's got her hands full, she's carrying a baby and her purse and her packages. So she puts her baby on top of the car, and she puts her purse on top of the car, and unloads her packages. Puts them in the car, takes her purse off the top of the car, and then she gets in, starts the car, and starts backing out of the . . . uh . . . parking spot and driving away. And the baby's on top just looking around, like, "Oh, this is fun," you know.

And she's, you know, starting to drive out of the parking lot, and there's this guy running after her screaming, "Hey, lady! Hey, lady!" pointing at the top of her car. And . . . um . . . next thing you know, there's like ten people running after her car, all yelling and screaming.

She's just driving along, and . . . uh . . . then thankfully, this truck, this delivery truck . . . uh . . . pulled out in front of her, and, you know, so she had to stop. And people are banging on her window. And she rolls down her window. "What? What's wrong?" And they hand her her baby, and she's just in a state of shock.

Next thing you know, everybody was laughing it off, but . . . wow – the baby was fine, by the way, the baby was totally fine. Crying and all, but it was fine. It really happened. True story!

2 Listen again

1. Play the stories again, pausing after each story so students can compare their answers.

2. Ask students to give their reactions to the stories.

3. Play one story again as a "model" for the storytelling in Activity D. Let students decide which one they'd most like to hear again.

Answers
Story 1: 4, 2, 3, 1
Story 2: 3, 2, 1, 4
Story 3: 2, 4, 3, 1

Activity C Pair work
page 70

Have students work in pairs. You may want to bring additional comic strips to class.

Activity D Communication task
page 70

Procedure

1. Be sure to look at Task 20 on page C-12 before the lesson so that you can answer any questions that may arise.

2. Divide the class into an even number of groups.

3. Circulate around the class as each group looks at the picture on page C-12 and works out a story to explain the scene.

4. Have two groups combine to compare their stories.

Follow-up activity

1. Ask students to look back through Lessons 1 through 30 in their books and decide which was their favorite lesson.

2. Ask each student to tell the class which was his or her favorite lesson and why.

Writing activity

Give students the following directions for a writing task:

Write one of the stories you heard in Activity B in your own words.

Review puzzles

The vocabulary in Puzzle A is from Lessons 27–28. The vocabulary in Puzzle B is from Lessons 29–30.

Puzzle A

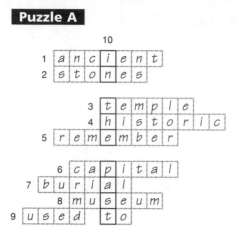

```
                    10
               1  a n c i e n t
               2  s t o n e s

           3  t e m p l e
           4  h i s t o r i c
         5  r e m e m b e r

             6  c a p i t a l
           7  b u r i a l
               8  m u s e u m
         9  u s e d   t o
```

Puzzle B

```
                         11
                    1  c a r t o o n
               2  h i l a r i o u s
                    3  c o m i c
               4  g i g g l e d
                 5  c o m e d i a n
                 6  s t o r y

                7  s e n s e
             8  l a u g h
                   9  j o k e s
             10  c l o w n
```

Key to communication tasks in Student's Book

Lesson	Activity	Student A	Student B	Student C
1	Describing someone's personality	Task 1/C-2	Task 12/C-8	
5	Role-playing in a restaurant	Task 2/C-2	Task 13/C-8	Task 13/C-8
7	Describing people	Task 3/C-3	Task 14/C-9	
9	Describing jobs	Task 4/C-3	Task 11/C-7	Task 15/C-9
11	Talking about inventions	Task 5/C-4	Task 10/C-7	Task 16/C-10
13	Talking about the environment	Task 8/C-6	Task 17/C-10	
14*	Talking about vacations	Task 6/C-4	Task 9/C-6	
16*	Learning about countries	Task 7/C-5	Task 18/C-11	
17	Talking about hobbies	Task 19/C-12	Task 29/C-17	
20	Pretending to be a famous person	Task 24/C-15	Task 28/C-16	Task 33/C-19
22†	Describing a scene from memory	Task 25/C-15	Task 25/C-15	
23	Learning about cities	Task 23/C-14	Task 31/C-18	
25†	Talking about paintings	Task 27/C-16	Task 27/C-16	
27	Telling a story	Task 21/C-13	Task 32/C-19	
29	Telling jokes	Task 22/C-13	Task 26/C-15	Task 30/C-17
30	Creating a story	Task 20/C-12	Task 20/C-12	Task 20/C-12

* In these activities two pairs of students work together. One pair turns to the first task. The other pair turns to the second task.

† In these activities both students turn to the same task.

113